RISING CLASS

How Three First-Generation College Students Conquered Their First Year

RISING CLASS

How Three First-Generation College Students Conquered Their First Year

JENNIFER MILLER

FARRAR STRAUS GIROUX
NEW YORK

Farrar Straus Giroux Books for Young Readers
An imprint of Macmillan Publishing Group, LLC
120 Broadway, New York, NY 10271 • fiercereads.com

Our books may be purchased in bulk for promotional, educational, or
business use. Please contact your local bookseller or the Macmillan Corporate
and Premium Sales Department at (800) 221-7945 ext. 5442 or by email at
MacmillanSpecialMarkets@macmillan.com.

Library of Congress Cataloging-in-Publication Data is available.

First edition, 2023
Book design by Samira Iravani
Printed in the United States of America

ISBN 978-0-374-31357-9 (hardcover)
1   3   5   7   9   10   8   6   4   2

For Fenn and Collin

Author's Note

Rising Class is a work of nonfiction based on three years of in-depth reporting. Though it primarily focuses on the experiences of Briani, Jacklynn, and Conner during their freshman year of college, I met them many months before they stepped foot on their respective campuses and continued to follow them long after their freshman year concluded. The process of getting to know them included visiting their hometowns and schools, meeting their friends and families, watching videos they took of their lives, and reading both the social posts and journal entries they shared with me. It was a process of developing deep relationships with all of them and, over many months, earning their trust.

That trust is crucial for any reporter, but in this case, it prompted me to make a series of decisions about how I would report and, ultimately, usher this book into existence. First, though everything you will read is true, it is not meant to be an objective accounting of events. There are multiple sides to every story, but this story belongs to Briani, Jacklynn, Conner, and a handful of their friends. It is the world through their eyes, interpreted by them. (I have changed the names and a handful of identifying details of some sources who did not participate directly in the telling of the story.)

Second, in fact-checking this book, I shared the manuscript with my primary sources and a handful of secondary characters before publication. That's not standard practice for a journalist, but I wanted to ensure that the students saw themselves reflected accurately and honestly in these pages. If anything wasn't right, we revised or removed it. In fact, they asked me to change very little. I believe that's a reflection of how well I came to know and understand them, but it's also a testament to their courage. The young adults in this book are not fictional characters. They are real people, making their way in the world (at this very moment!), trying to figure it all out. But they were incredibly vulnerable because they knew that being so might help others understand the first-gen experience. I hope their stories will move, inspire, and challenge you as they did me.

PROLOGUE

BRIANI

Bin Drama

Briani stood in the line of students at Hartley Hall, sweating in her oversized button-down shirt and jeans. Her flight was first thing tomorrow, and her room was only half-packed.

But this wasn't just anxiety sweat; this was four-alarm-fire sweat. Not because of the invisible and highly contagious virus sweeping the city. No, Briani was sweating because she couldn't find her moving bin.

The World Health Organization had just declared Covid-19 a pandemic. As a result, colleges across the country were shuttering their campuses and kicking out their students. Including Briani.

But the moving bin, which she needed to physically remove her belongings from her dorm room, was only free for the first two hours. Return your bin late, and you had to pay Columbia Housing $70 a day. Lose your bin, and you had to pay them $350.

Briani did not have $350.

Another student might think, *This sucks, but worst case, I'll ask my parents for help.*

Briani didn't know if her parents could spare $350. But it didn't matter. She would never ask them for that kind of money.

She reached the front of the line. "Hi," she said to the lady from Residential Life. "I'm sorry, but I misplaced my bin."

Was it even worth explaining that it wasn't her fault? That in any other circumstance, Briani wouldn't have left $350 worth of anything just sitting around? But she lived on the fifteenth floor of John Jay Hall—the only floor without an elevator. And at her meager 5'3", she couldn't exactly pull a 120-gallon bin up the flight of stairs to her room, let alone get it back down again, piled with everything she owned. So she'd left the bin by the staircase on fourteen.

Only when she returned with her first load of boxes, the bin was gone.

The housing woman looked at the line of students behind Briani, eager to keep things moving. "If it's signed out to you, then it's on you," she said.

SHIT! Briani ran back to her dorm. She was seriously freaking. She jumped on her floor's group chat and put out an APB for the bin on Instagram.

Her friend Monroe was kind enough to rent her a second bin, because Briani still had to move out. Finally, hours later, she got everything out of the dorm. She looked at the pile: eleven boxes representing the six most momentous months of her life, unceremoniously sitting on the sidewalk. It was not the ending she'd imagined for her freshman year of college at Columbia University in the City of New York.

Briani's aunt Titi Jackie was there, wearing a mask. She was too afraid to enter the building and had been sitting outside for more than an hour. Together, they pushed the bin to the street and called an Uber. Briani counted herself lucky; Titi Jackie lived in Washington Heights, many blocks north of campus. She'd be storing her niece's things for however long school was closed.

But when they packed the Uber, the car only had room for a single passenger. "I love you Titi, but take this. Bye-bye!" Briani gave her aunt a hug. She felt terrible, sending Titi Jackie away in the car by herself. But what could she do? They weren't going to pay for two Ubers. And anyway, she still needed to find the missing bin.

Briani checked her phone. Someone said they'd seen a bin over on frat row, so she ran over. Nothing. Her phone was about to die. She was frustrated, upset, about to lose her mind. She rushed back to her dorm.

Her side of room 1513 was barren, like she'd never even lived there.

She plugged in her phone, sat down at her desk. For once it wasn't a mess of books and highlighters and mugs of cold tea.

Someone knocked on the door. It was a kid from her floor, short, always quiet, nobody she knew well.

"Hey," he said. "I heard you were looking for your bin?"

Briani nodded, hopeful.

"I took it to help somebody. I didn't know it was checked out. I can return it when I'm finished. I'm so sorry."

Relief swept through her. *God bless.* She wasn't out a small fortune.

It was past midnight, and she needed to be up before dawn, so she pulled on her comfy plane clothes: baggy overalls and her baby-blue Columbia University sweatshirt. Her sheets and blanket were packed, so she curled up, her cheek pressed to the bare mattress.

But she couldn't sleep. The room was too quiet, like she could feel the campus slowly draining of life. She'd worked so hard to get here. And not just her but her family.

Her father had trekked across the Mexican border at fourteen.

Her mother had left the Dominican Republic to forge a new life in America.

They'd poured their sweat into the family restaurant.

Her mother had waylaid her own college dreams to provide for the family.

Briani had spent years studying and building her résumé, praying and serving the community, pulling her weight with after-school and weekend jobs—all to make college possible.

When Columbia accepted her, her joy had been the purest kind.

Now, as she lay there, Briani's relief turned to anger. Because she was getting kicked out of school, obviously. But also because of that stupid moving bin. Because every single bin was signed out to a specific person. The kid from her floor knew it, and he took hers anyway.

He hadn't thought for a second about the panic he'd caused her. Or what would have happened had he lost her bin and left her on the hook for $350. It had taken months, but she'd finally found a home here—no, *built* a home here. And yet even in leaving, she was reminded of the gulf between herself and so many other students. They all lived on the same campus, but they didn't live in the same world.

Now Briani was being thrown back into that world, everything upended. And for how long?

Nobody knew.

SUMMER 2019

BRIANI

Kiwanis Club

In Lawrenceville, Georgia, the July sun was unrelenting. It wasn't super comfortable for a picnic, but Briani was making the most of her remaining time here. Most of her besties from Mountainview High School were going to Georgia State University in Atlanta, about forty miles away. Some were even rooming together. They could picnic together whenever they wanted.

Briani wasn't just leaving the state. She was heading to an Ivy League college in Manhattan, one of the world's most cosmopolitan (not to mention expensive) cities. Her friends were genuinely excited for her. Their girl was the first person in her family to attend a four-year college. It was a huge risk and a very big deal.

But that didn't stop them from ribbing her about her "bougie" tastes. Like the Birkenstocks on her feet. "*You paid $125 for those!?!*" They gawked as they laid out a patchwork of blankets and unpacked a small grocery store feast: soda, chips, and sliced fruit.

Briani was indignant. She'd folded clothes at Old Navy, saving for months—*months!*—to afford the Birks. "I got that paycheck and I was like, I deserve this," she said. And it wasn't like she was bougie head to toe. Her thrifted Old Navy tee with the American flag had cost her, what, three bucks?

Yeah, the others replied, but what about your MacBook?

"That came from a scholarship!"

And your Apple Watch?

She admitted she'd asked for the watch as a graduation gift. "My parents didn't even know what a graduation gift *was*," she said. "They were like, You graduated. *That's* your gift."

The other first-gen kids in the group laughed. Getting a present for completing your education would be like getting a present for waking up in the morning.

"I don't want first-generation and low income to define everything I am," Briani said, palming a couple of chips. "But how can it not when kids at Columbia wear thousand-dollar Canada Goose?"

"Canada who?" asked Denescia, who was going to GSU.

"One-thousand-dollar parkas," said Briani's best friend, Maia, who was also going to GSU.

Denescia's mouth dropped open.

"If I see any of those coats, I'll cry," Briani said. She looked like she was only half-joking.

Fancy coats aside, Briani couldn't wait for New York. She had nothing against Lawrenceville. It was a decent place to grow up. She had close friends, a loving family, and a supportive church. She'd learned how to navigate southern culture, which wasn't easy for the Latina daughter of immigrants. But that was the point: Too often, she had to contort herself to fit in. Or let uncomfortable things go. Like the cringey incident that very morning.

A few hours before the picnic, she'd put on a green dress and swapped her Birks for a pair of block-heel sandals. She was receiving a scholarship for her high school community service work from a local Kiwanis Club. The ceremony was held at a community center in nearby Sugar Hill. It had started okay. There was a prayer, super typical. Then an inspirational speech from one of the Kiwanis leaders, a middle-aged white dude. Also typical.

"You've been given a gift and it's your responsibility to pay it forward," he told Briani and the other scholarship recipients. It was the kind of cliché adults loved, but Briani liked this guy. For over a year now, he'd been wonderfully supportive of her service work.

The Kiwanis leader continued, "In thirty years, I expect you to be standing up here instead of me. Because in thirty years, I'll probably be shot by the husband of a twenty-year-old."

Okay, what now?

"Oh, I'll keep you in line," joked the man's wife, gamely playing along.

Briani just smiled through her discomfort.

The Kiwanis leader was unfazed. "There's a student who couldn't be here today," he said. "She's an immigrant who overcame a significant language barrier." Then he looked directly at Briani—American-born Briani—as though one Latina student was interchangeable from the next, and said, "It's so cool that you weren't only learning science and algebra but doing so in a *foreign* language."

Briani's smile did not waver. Her body did not stiffen. She'd perfected the art of Southern agreeability.

After the ceremony, Briani had lunch at Jalapeño Mexican Restaurant, which her parents owned in a Lawrenceville strip mall. *The Business*, as the family called it, had a cheerful, casual vibe. BIENVENIDOS!! exclaimed a large hand-drawn sign above the kitchen pass-through window. Briani had spent countless hours here helping her parents, hanging with friends, and doing homework.

"Yeah, yeah, yeah," she said about the Kiwanis Club leader, like his speech was no surprise. "He doesn't know my whole story. Being in the South, it's one of those things . . ."

It had been "one of those things" for as long as she could remember. When she first moved to town at age five, the school put her in ESL classes. She wasn't just fluent in English; she was bilingual. Her parents complained, and the school tested her for the gifted program. She'd been in gifted classes ever since.

"It's one of those things," she repeated. "People here, they just assume. They don't always know better." She said the man from Kiwanis had good intentions. He'd done a lot for her, connecting her with local nonprofits, supporting her projects. "What can I do?" She sighed. "I can try to educate or be forgiving."

But maybe New York would feel like a relief. Maybe in the city, there wouldn't be quite so much to forgive.

CONNER & JACKLYNN

Best Regards

Conner and Jacklynn, a couple of two and a half years, stood outside the Heartland Brewery in Times Square and perused the menu. "This should be fine," Conner decided. "As long as we don't get the steak."

The steak was a big-ticket item, as steaks generally are. And though their school trip down the East Coast included a meal stipend, that amount seemed better calibrated to the price of food where they'd come from (Missouri) than to the price of food in the place they were visiting (Manhattan).

They entered, neither one considering the irony: Two white teenagers from the actual heartland had chosen a restaurant designed to evoke middle America, located in the heart of New York City.

Jacklynn pulled off her bright yellow poncho and shook out her long brown ponytail. She'd never been to New York before and was touristing hard, complete with a fanny pack and a T-shirt that read BROOKLYN. Conner had gifted her the shirt earlier that year, delivering it on the back of a human-sized teddy bear they'd seen in Goodwill. He'd even thought to spray the shirt with his deodorant, an Old Spice scent called Bearglove. This way, she could remember what he smelled like when they were apart.

A month from now, Conner would return to New York City for his freshman year at Columbia University. Jacklynn would go to Ozarks Technical Community College back home. They were both the first in their families to go to college, but they would soon be separated by nearly 1,200 miles. They were trying not to think about it.

"I'm very in awe of everything I'm seeing," Jacklynn said, reflecting on their afternoon. "I love all the lights here, all the color."

"The city that never sleeps," Conner said. He had a way of leaning into clichés, treating them with a kind of ironic reverence. By appearance, he looked less the tourist than Jacklynn. He wore a white T-shirt under a red windbreaker, gray Chucks, and an asymmetrical haircut that was half close shave, half flop of brown. But his loping walk gave him away. He had not yet developed the brisk gait of New York City locals.

Not that either of them cared how they looked. They were too excited to be visiting Broadway together. They'd fallen for each other during a high school production of *Charlie and the Chocolate Factory*, when Conner played the gluttonous Golden Ticket winner Augustus Gloop and Jacklynn played Augustus's fawning mother. One day, in the middle of rehearsal, Conner turned toward Jacklynn after making a joke. Suddenly, she was smitten.

"I saw his blue eyes and I thought, This kid is awesome," she said.

"I thought you'd been funny the *whole* time," Conner said.

Jacklynn rolled her eyes. Their dynamic was one of frequent, playful joshing. Their connection grew from a love of all things geeky, from a progressive worldview that was iconoclastic for rural Ozark, Missouri, and for their difficult upbringing.

They'd both been raised by loving single mothers. They both grew up in homes devastated by addiction.

Conner's dad died from an overdose when he was three.

Jacklynn's dad, whom she hadn't seen for five years, struggled with alcoholism. (His absence was, she admitted, something of a relief.)

As a result, neither of them touched substances of any kind.

As a result, they shouldered a lot of responsibility.

"I credit seventy-five to eighty percent of my maturity level to my relationship with my father and dealing with things in my life," Jacklynn said. She nodded at Conner. "It's the same for you."

"I only pay for dinner at home sometimes," Conner said.

"Don't discredit yourself for what you've paid for," Jacklynn said.

"When we first moved into our current house, it was every night for a few weeks," Conner conceded. "My mother's carried a lot of weight."

Conner's mom, Stacey, was thirteen years sober, but she suffered from post-traumatic stress disorder and had difficulty holding down a steady job. Conner and his younger brother, Ayden, were supported by their mom's monthly disability checks, frequent help from their grandparents, and assistance from whatever boyfriend Stacey happened to be living with. When a relationship ended (as it just had), the whole family would be forced to move, and things always grew kind of precarious. Hence Conner helping to pay for dinner with earnings from the serving and dishwashing job he held at a local coffee shop.

For him, Columbia was an opportunity to start something fresh, something all his own. He was the only person from his friend group to leave the state for school, but it was a risk he was willing to take.

Their food arrived, and Jacklynn began picking the tomatoes off her buffalo burger. She'd asked for no tomatoes, but obviously, the server wasn't paying attention. She could empathize—in Missouri, she worked at a restaurant called Big Whiskey's, and sometimes your mind was just elsewhere. On the other hand, she hated tomatoes.

Conner was eating a Greek salad, also removing the tomatoes. Watching him, Jacklynn felt protective. Of course, he could take care of himself. He'd been doing that while also helping to support his family emotionally and financially for years. But he was also allergic to confrontation. Jacklynn didn't want people taking advantage of him.

For example, last month, he'd received an email from a guy named Rob. *Hello Connor*, Rob had written, misspelling Conner's name. *I was assigned as your roommate. There is a mix-up because I'm supposed to room with a member of the handball team since I'm coming in as a new recruit. If you could please do me a huge favor and email housing and ask them to specifically swap rooms with the name "Thomas Marshall" as soon as possible that would be amazing. Thank you. Best regards. Rob.*

"Best regards," Jacklynn scoffed as she chewed her burger.

"That's the part that gets me every time. It's like, Hey, I don't want to house with you, best regards."

Conner reddened, partly from embarrassment and partly because his baby-faced cheeks were perpetually flushed. Dutifully, he'd contacted the housing office, which then asked him to provide Thomas's email. So Conner went looking for Thomas's email but couldn't find it. So he'd gone back to Rob. After a while, Rob wrote to say that he didn't need Conner's help after all. Housing was on the case. *They already confirmed the switch with me*, Rob wrote. *Hope everything gets sorted out. Cheers.*

Conner replied, *Thanks! Yeah, I'm sure it's fine. Are you getting excited for orientation?*

Rob never responded.

Now, three weeks later, Conner still hadn't received any information about where he was living or who his new roommate was. "I thought, Maybe Rob's from a different country and needed someone from the handball team to help him acclimate," Conner said. "But my friends Googled him, and they said he went to a well-known prep school." Conner paused, considered. "He could be a perfectly nice guy."

Jacklynn wasn't buying this. "It's like the college scandal," she said. She was referring to Operation Varsity Blues. Earlier that year, the FBI had discovered that wealthy parents, including Aunt Becky from *Full House*, had paid hundreds of thousands of dollars to buy their kids spots at prestigious universities. In some cases, these parents had forged their kids' applications, photoshopping images of them playing varsity sports like crew. Jacklynn shook her head. "That email from Rob is like, Please email the school and tell them I need to be catered to immediately."

"It's going to be fine," Conner said. "I'm not too worried about it."

The server arrived to take their plates and asked if they wanted dessert. Conner looked at the menu. "We'll have a slice of your *New York*–style cheesecake," he said, reading verbatim. He knew the dessert would likely be nothing special—that the name was designed to upsell tourists like them. But he was an optimist, and there was always the chance, however small, that the cake could be more: delicious, even phenomenal.

FIRST
SEMESTER

FAQS: COLUMBIA UNIVERSITY

WHAT IS IT?

A four-year, private, nonprofit school that offers both under-graduate and graduate fields of study. The graduate programs make Columbia a university, instead of just a college. This also means that many classes are taught by underpaid graduate students who may or may not have previous teaching experience.

WHERE'S IT LOCATED?

116th Street and Broadway on the Upper West Side of Manhattan. The thirty-six-acre campus of stately buildings, verdant greens, and brick pathways is tucked between Riverside Park to the West, Morningside Park to the East, Manhattan Valley to the South, and West Harlem to the North. People call it an urban oasis, which is pretty accurate. Within ten minutes, you can walk to Central Park; within five seconds, you can walk to Shake Shack.

HOW OLD IS IT?

In 1754, King George II of England opened King's College in lower Manhattan. After shuttering during the Revolutionary War, the school reopened in 1784 as Columbia University. Despite a hand-ful of newly constructed and renovated buildings, much of cam-pus feels like it hasn't been updated since the late 1800s.

WHAT DOES IT MEAN TO BE AN 'IVY LEAGUE' SCHOOL?

The Ivy League is really just an athletic conference. Harvard, Yale, Princeton, Brown, Dartmouth, the University of Pennsylvania, Cornell, and Columbia all compete against one another. But the schools are more widely known for their rigor and exclusivity. In 2018, when Conner and Briani applied to Columbia, 42,569 students vied for a spot. The university accepted just 5.1 percent of them.

HOW MUCH DOES IT COST?

In 2019, the sticker price for tuition and fees was $61,788, plus $14,490 for room and board, $1,294 for books and supplies, and $2,180 for other expenses, according to the National Center for Education Statistics. But most students don't pay anywhere near that. Columbia is committed to covering 100 percent of demonstrated family need. During the 2020–2021 school year, though the total cost of attendance was $82,585, half of Columbia students received an average grant from the university in the amount of $68,250. Students aren't expected to borrow any money to attend Columbia.

WHO GOES THERE?

Briani and Conner's freshmen year, there were about nine thousand undergrads, including engineering students and adult learners returning to school. Just over half were students of color, and 18 percent were the first in their families to attend college. Almost all of them were full-time students living on campus as freshmen.

WHAT DO UNDERGRADS STUDY?

Columbia is known for its Core Curriculum of six mandatory courses. These are Literature Humanities (Lit Hum), Contemporary Civilizations (CC), University Writing (UW), Art Humanities, Music Humanities, and Frontiers of Science (Fro Sci).

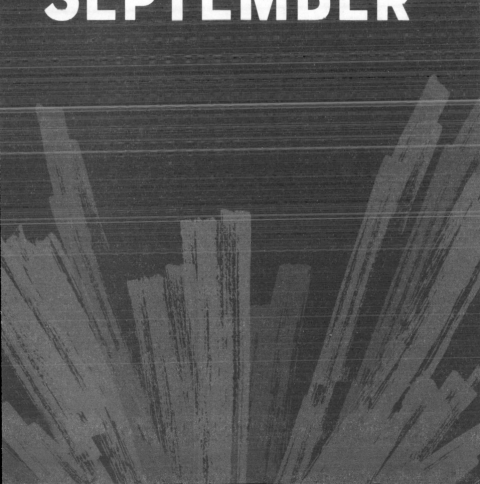

AUGUST/
SEPTEMBER

CONNER

The Night Before

Conner was starting to feel nervous. He was excited to see his dorm and meet the roommate he'd (finally) been assigned. But standing in his Times Square hotel room, he suddenly understood just how far he was from home. Homesickness wasn't something he'd anticipated.

His grandparents were asleep in the same hotel room. They'd be helping him settle in tomorrow. He loved them, but it wasn't the same as having his mom or Jacklynn by his side.

Yesterday, back in Springfield, Missouri, he'd gone bowling with them and his little brother, Ayden. Then his friends had gathered for pizza and *Spaceballs*. All too soon, it was time to take Jacklynn home; it was super late, and Conner hadn't started packing.

They drove in silence. The car felt strangely empty, like she wasn't sitting beside him. At her house, they sat in the car and discussed all the expected things. They promised to talk every day. They promised to use the "long distance" bracelets Jacklynn had bought—wrist bands that lit up and vibrated to let the other person know you were thinking of them. They said they'd mail a journal back and forth. They reminded each other that in a few short months, Conner would be home for Thanksgiving.

They walked together to the front door. Conner made a bunch of bad jokes to lighten the mood. Jacklynn did not laugh at any of them.

They pulled each other close.

As Conner drove away, he began to cry. He could see Jacklynn standing at her front door, waving him off like always. This time, though, she was still there when he reached the end of the street. "We really milked it," he said.

Conner was a film buff; he had an eye for a great final shot.

In fact, this was only the penultimate goodbye. The next morning, an entire entourage saw him off: Stacey and Ayden; Jacklynn and her mom, Sherry; her sister Crystal; her brother-in-law, Jake; and her two-and-a-half-year-old niece. That's how important this moment was. That's how much they loved Conner.

Conner was mostly focused on making sure Jacklynn was okay. He bought her a toy chicken at the gift shop—an inside joke from their theater days—and she clutched it as he walked through security. "Jacklynn was pretty solid at the end," he said.

Now in his hotel room, Conner felt less solid. Or maybe he was just running on three hours of sleep, which is what happens when you pack for college literally hours before your flight departs.

Deep down, he knew that everything was going to be fine.

He looked out over Times Square. This kind of height didn't exist in Missouri unless you were a pilot or a bird.

Tomorrow was going to be great.

BRIANI

Move-in Day

Briani chose her move-in outfit for maximum comfort: a black Nike T-shirt, athletic shorts, and of course, her Birkenstocks. It was late August in Manhattan, and the humidity was so thick it shimmered.

Her dorm, John Jay Hall, was fifteen red-brick floors with white-trimmed windows on the eastern edge of Columbia's main campus. It seemed like she'd been in and out of it a dozen times already, pulling bags, pushing bins, grabbing snacks. Each time she entered, she passed a large blue sign that said WELCOME TO COLUMBIA. MAKE IT YOUR HOME. Everyone was certainly trying; all around her, students maneuvered industrial blue moving bins piled with their worldly belongings.

Briani had been assigned a room on the dorm's top floor, which some kids were calling "the penthouse."

This was misleading.

Briani quickly discovered her floor lacked key features, like a student lounge and an elevator. That meant she had to park her bin on the floor below and carry everything—*everything!*—up the stairs. At least she had help. Her dad, José, and her first cousin, Alberto, were helping her move in.

Alberto, tall and skinny with a mess of curls, was the closest

Briani had to a college guide. He was a rising junior at Cornell. He was raised by his father—a New York City police officer—who hadn't gone to college, either. By now, though, he knew the routine. He could tell Briani things like, "Keep your door open so you'll seem more inviting," and, "If you have a problem with financial aid, make sure you actually call the office. Emails will disappear into a black hole."

José did not know the routine and sat quietly at his daughter's desk. He would have felt better with Briani's mom, Leonor, there. But one of them had to stay home and run the restaurant. The previous fall, right as Briani was applying to college, Leonor was laid off from her managerial position with the local health department. So closing the restaurant even temporarily was not an option. And Leonor was struggling to keep up with her own schooling—the online bachelor's degree that she'd been chipping away at for years.

Throughout high school, Briani often worked on her mom's assignments before starting her own. Somehow, she managed to maintain a 4.3 GPA in her school's gifted and talented program, work twenty hours a week at Old Navy, and show up regularly to varsity tennis, yearbook committee, and community service clubs.

"I'm the first one doing all these things, the first one to go to college, the first to figure out financial aid and get everything in order," Briani said, standing among her half-unpacked suitcases. "It's super hard. I'm still kinda scared to do things on my own."

That fall, roughly a third of college students in the United States were first-generation. Most attended community colleges and public universities. A much smaller number went to private liberal arts schools and the Ivy League. But their numbers were increasing, and elite schools scrambled to draw more first-generation and low-income students—"FLI" students—to campus. They'd started paying these FLI students to promote the liberal arts experience back home. They'd opened dorms specifically for FLI students, hired FLI deans, and launched FLI orientation programs. They'd partnered with college-access organizations. Still, there was no substitute for having a parent who'd been to college or had the time and resources to become knowledgeable about the college process.

Leonor had an associate's degree. José had gotten his GED after coming to America as an undocumented teenager, crossing the border under the cover of night. When he was Briani's age, he was working the overnight shift at a Manhattan diner called Lox Around the Clock. He'd learned to make falafel and matzo ball soup. He could still bake a mean challah, but he'd never filled out the Common App (the standardized application that allows students to apply to nearly nine hundred colleges) or the Free Application for Federal Student Aid (FAFSA) or the College Scholarship Service Profile (CSS). Briani's parents didn't have time to work on these applications; and why should they? They weren't the ones applying.

Briani had to figure out what was required, ask her parents to dig it up, and then fill out the forms herself. One mistake could upend everything.

This, the girl who said she was afraid to do things on her own.

"She's breaking the circle," José said. "Even in Mexico, my family only went through the sixth grade."

As Briani unpacked, she and Alberto discussed her financial aid situation. An email from the school said she was being charged $2,000 a semester plus the cost of health insurance. Apparently, they'd failed to apply the community service scholarship she'd received. Briani was stressed about this. She needed that money to pay off her Student Responsibility, an annual fee between $2,400 and $3,400, required of all students, even those who, like Briani, had received full financial aid. If she couldn't pay, she might not be allowed to register for classes.

A lot of FLI kids were having similar issues. Alberto said that Cornell had just sent him a $12,000 bill out of nowhere.

There was a knock at the door. In walked a skinny woman with a half ponytail of wavy hair and an effusive smile. This was Leonor's sister Jackie, known to her niece as Titi Jackie.

Briani rushed into Titi Jackie's arms.

"I brought you some things," Titi Jackie said. Her voice had a cooing, almost gushing quality, as though the world were a big, adorable baby. She handed Briani two bags from Marshalls and watched with anticipation as her niece pulled items from the cellophane: a peony-scented candle, a prayer journal stamped with the words THIS GIRL HAS GOALS, a key chain featuring the Dominican Republic flag, a miniature succulent.

It was true that none of these objects quite matched the "Bedroom Goals" Pinterest board Briani had been keeping since high school. But given her basically nonexistent budget, Titi Jackie's generosity seriously warmed her heart.

"And one more thing," Titi Jackie said. She handed Briani a mug that said I LOVE MOM.

"This is gonna make me cry," Briani said, and started crying.

Titi Jackie pulled out both regular and travel-sized Kleenex.

Briani wiped at her eyes. "Before I left, I teased my mom, 'You're gonna miss me.' But I miss her so much."

"You're making *me* cry," Titi Jackie said, also crying. She pulled Briani into her slender arms. "I love you so much, princess."

José looked on awkwardly, swelling with pride for his oldest child and her courage. He busied himself cleaning up the wrapping paper.

Briani broke away from her aunt and took stock of the unfinished room. There was so much to do. She made her bed but then realized her pillow was directly under the dormer ceiling. "If I try to sit up, I'll hit my head!" she exclaimed. She started pulling up the sheets to make the bed the other way.

CONNER

Should I Stay or Should I Go

Conner woke up at 8:00 a.m., threw on a Ramones T-shirt, khaki shorts, and the BOSTON baseball cap he'd purchased while traveling with Jacklynn last month. Then he and his grandparents caught a taxi to campus.

He hadn't expected Stacey to help him move. He knew the stress of the trip, not to mention the city, would be challenging for her. For instance, his mom was convinced he'd be mowed down by a subway train. But Stacey had also been having a difficult time these last few months.

Because of her breakup.

Because Conner was leaving.

Because after thirteen years of sobriety, she'd had "one relapse."

He was pretty sure she'd be fine. Still, he wished she could have been here. His mom had raised him, had been there for him. She'd first introduced him to the Ramones, to the Clash, to most of his musical tastes. They always had music in the car: driving to and from school or, on the weekends, exploring flea markets and secondhand stores. They'd sing along, nodding their heads to "Should I Stay or Should I Go."

Conner had also lobbied for Ayden to come along. He was

thirteen and on the autism spectrum. Conner believed a trip to New York would help expand his horizons, make him feel special. But his grandparents said it would make things overly complicated, so Ayden stayed home with Stacey.

Campus was a chaotic symphony of cheering upperclassmen, thumping hip-hop, and growling lawn mowers. Streams of new arrivals and their parents wandered by looking very lost. Conner and his grandparents found their way to Carman Hall, his dorm, another red-brick building on the school's main campus. They then followed the line of students waiting to enter as it wound down two flights of steps, out onto the sidewalk, down the block, and around the corner. Apparently, one of the elevators was broken, so things were moving slowly. Conner brought his make-the-best-of-things optimism to the situation:

On the upside, he was only on the second floor, so he didn't really need the elevator.

On the downside, the second floor had not been renovated in years and was kind of a dump.

On the upside, his actual room (when he finally arrived there) had an impressive amount of closet space and even a recycling bin. For Conner this was exciting; it was the kind of unnecessary expense his mom wouldn't have considered.

On the downside, his room didn't have much of a view, just the side of a large building.

On the upside, the large building was nice looking.

His grandfather seemed to think the room was just fine. His

grandma was more skeptical; shouldn't an Ivy League dorm be a little nicer? At the very least, she said, she'd make his bed for him later. She didn't trust his bed-making skills, and she wanted him to get a good night's sleep.

Conner dropped his bags. He didn't really feel like unpacking, and his grandparents were eager to get some sightseeing in.

A few hours later, Conner headed toward a welcome tent offering free lunch. Two girls crossed his path, one of them carrying a tennis racket. "What do you like better, this or Yale?" she asked her friend. In short succession, he passed another girl dressed head to toe in Chanel.

None of that was interesting to him. Here's what was: Bottle Guy—a skinny man wearing head-to-toe spandex and a balaclava, who often stood on the plaza below Low Memorial Library, trying to throw a water bottle into a trash can . . . with his feet.

"That's not something I've seen before," Conner said, as though more experienced New Yorkers might find this sight merely quotidian.

But Bottle Guy represented precisely the weird stuff that excited Conner. He couldn't wait to join Columbia's Science Fiction Society and the Philolexian Society, an absurdist literary club. "And I know this will all seem just like normal," he said, "but pigeons! There are so many of them, and they will come right up to you."

Pigeons and Bottle Guy: the simple, if extraordinary, things Conner didn't have in Ozark, Missouri.

After lunch, Conner headed back to his dorm to finish unpacking. Out came a book by the writer-director David Mamet, which he'd stolen from a high school teacher, who had previously stolen it from the Ozark High School library. "Secondhand theft doesn't really count," Conner said. From a single brown boot, he extracted a small jewelry box. It had been his mom's suggestion to hide his keepsakes there. "I bought the box at an antique store," he said. "By which I mean Goodwill." Inside he had a promposal gift from Jacklynn and small rubber chicken that he snagged from a Springfield bowling alley. He said his family had been banned from the establishment a decade ago, after his mother's then boyfriend got drunk and cussed out management.

Conner set his seventeen-inch Dell laptop on the desk. He didn't have a lock for it, but it was quite heavy, so maybe would-be thieves wouldn't bother? He said he was hoping to keep his door open, as he'd heard it created social opportunities—if his roommate didn't mind.

After the Rob handball debacle, Conner had been paired with an international student named Omar. He seemed nice, Conner said, and he hoped they could watch movies together.

Conner believed that sitting through *Children of Men* or *Scott Pilgrim vs. the World* or even the laughably terrible (but thoroughly enjoyable!) *Waterworld* with your friends was a perfect shared experience. He loved that when a movie ended, everybody felt a similar fusion of melancholy and euphoria.

Still, he didn't want to seem overeager. If he threw *Waterworld* at his new friends, they might question his sanity. Better to start with a legit crowd-pleaser like *Dr. Strangelove*.

Of course, first Conner needed to meet people. And right now, there wasn't really anyone around. So he'd unpack. See if Omar returned. Maybe talk to Jacklynn when she got off work at Big Whiskey's. Conner also suspected he'd hear from his mother. Stacey had already called once, but a second and possibly third time was likely on the horizon. "I know that I'm going to be fine without her, and she'll be fine without me," he said. "But she doesn't know that."

BRIANI

New Student Orientation Program Aka NSOP

Every day during NSOP and for many days afterward, Briani woke up with a lump in her throat. Orientation week had a mantra: *Can't Stop, Won't Stop, NSOP!* It was like careening around curves in a race car, and she didn't know how to drive. Like freshman year of high school all over again. Every day there was pressure: to choose classes, pick clubs, make friends. Just having someone to sit with at lunch felt like a challenge. She wasn't gonna lie. Her anxiety was intense.

Take the dumpster fire that was class registration. By the time her slot came up, nearly every course she wanted had a waitlist.

Or she'd just be walking through campus and happen to see a kid rush by in Gucci sneakers. And she'd suddenly be reminded that this was Columbia, and she was now living in Manhattan, and kids on campus could afford things like that.

Or she'd be out with some new kids she'd met, exploring Times Square (which, btw, was crazy crowded and smelled like pee). And afterward they'd grab food from Chick-fil-A. And halfway through her small cone and fries, the homesickness would hit. So she'd call her mom, who made her feel better but also like crying.

Or she'd have a list of FLI and Latinx activities to attend, any of which could be her ticket to new friends. But she didn't go, because she was overwhelmed, and her laundry was piling up, and she still hadn't bought half of her school supplies.

But then something would happen—some small thing—and it would renew her faith. *Yes, I can do this. Yes, I'm meant to be here.* Like the girl she went to lunch with after the mandatory Academic Integrity session (takeaway: don't plagiarize!), who'd gone to a Manhattan private school but was super chill and down-to-earth.

Or the night she'd gone with some FLI kids to a party in Carman (not her scene!) and afterward, they'd all come over to *her* room to hang.

Or posters she'd bought from a kiosk on the street, which turned her room from blank slate to a semblance of home.

Or the floor dinner where she met Genevieve, the first person who might actually become a friend.

FAQS: OZARKS TECHNICAL COMMUNITY COLLEGE

WHAT IS IT?

A public community college offering two-year associate's degrees and certificates in technical and vocational programs. At OTC, you can study anything from turf-and-landscape management to physical therapy to culinary arts. From the sciences to liberal arts.

WHERE'S IT LOCATED?

There are six OTC campuses in southwestern Missouri. Jacklynn's freshman classes were held at the Richwood Valley site, an eighty-four-acre campus consisting of a 60,000-square-foot academic hub and a brand-new 8,000-square-foot agricultural education center and 2,400-square-foot greenhouse, plus meadows, woods, and a natural spring, right off a rural highway. Richwood Valley has an office park vibe, but also office park resources: ergonomic chairs, dry-erase markers flowing with ink (neither of which can be counted on at Columbia), and the ease of everything happening in one place.

HOW OLD IS IT? WHO STARTED IT?

OTC was founded in 1990 by the Springfield, Missouri, school district and thirteen surrounding public school districts.

ARE COMMUNITY COLLEGES LESS RIGOROUS THAN OTHER TYPES OF SCHOOLS?

They can be, but they are very much the beating heart of American higher education. About a third of all college students are first-generation, and most of them attend community colleges and other public schools.

SO WHY DO THEY HAVE A REPUTATION AS MEDIOCRE?

Because they don't offer a "classic" four-year liberal arts education. Because they're often underfunded. And because there's a lot of elitism in academia. Community colleges are about accessibility. To attend OTC, you don't need a transcript packed with AP and Honors classes. You certainly don't have to be a musical/athletic/intellectual phenom. And you don't need to be rich. Jacklynn's freshman year, OTC tuition and fees for in-state students were $4,763. Before scholarships and aid.

THAT SOUNDS GREAT. SO WHY WOULDN'T EVERYONE WANT TO GO?

Community college won't give you a campus-oriented collegiate experience. There are no dorms, sometimes no robust slate of student clubs and extracurriculars. Most people live at home; many attend school while working full- or part-time jobs or raising families. Since student bodies are hyperlocal, they tend to reflect local demographics. Only 18 percent of OTC students aren't white, and about a third are first-generation students.

WHAT'S BETTER—A COMMUNITY COLLEGE OR A TRADITIONAL FOUR-YEAR COLLEGE?

It depends on what you're looking for. Community college can help you access a four-year college or become certified in certain professional and vocational fields—many of them with healthy salaries. But you can't jump directly from community college into law school, medical school, or business school. An associate's degree probably won't get you hired by big-name tech and finance firms.

JACKLYNN

The Comforts of Home

Jacklynn's first day at OTC felt like any other day. She already had fifteen college credits under her belt through a high school dual-enrollment program, and OTC's Richwood campus was also super close to home. Which is to say, her mom would not be taking first-day photos on the front lawn. Two years from now, when she planned to transfer to Missouri State University, a bigger deal could be made.

"I know I shouldn't look down at the college I'm going to," Jacklynn said a few days into the semester. "But it's still community college, and classes might be a little easier."

The bigger change was the absence of Conner—and the fact that some people (e.g., her entire family) kept asking how she felt about him leaving.

How did she feel?

She'd watch a random video that reminded her of him and cry.

She'd be driving home from work and think about the upcoming fall activities she'd do without him. And cry.

She'd think about how many months remained until Thanksgiving. And then she'd cry.

She'd known for at least a year that he'd be leaving. She understood they were on different paths, and she was perfectly happy with the one she'd chosen. But that didn't fill the Conner-shaped hole in her heart.

When they met junior year, they were already on diverging academic paths. Conner was enrolled in Ozark High School's International Baccalaureate program. It was about as good a preparation for college as you could get, especially if you had your sights set on a place like Columbia.

Jacklynn took a couple of stand-alone IB classes in high school, but she'd opted for the state's A+ Scholarship Program, which would cover community college tuition and a decent chunk of MSU tuition if she maintained her GPA. "I got a lot more free things out of doing it this way," she said. That was important. Her sister had dropped out of a local private college because she couldn't afford it.

After they started dating, Conner suggested Jacklynn look into QuestBridge, the college-access program that had helped him attend Columbia. But the process of applying to QuestBridge, and then going through the program, and then researching out-of-state schools, and then actually having to leave home (which would *not* fly with her mom) was too complicated.

Jacklynn wanted to major in design, and MSU had a good program. That was enough for her.

She did wonder about the "typical" college experience, like living in a dorm. In the future, maybe she'd move to New York or California with Conner. He'd make movies and she'd design costumes. Then she thought about her best friend from high school, who now went to college in St. Louis, about three and a half hours away. "Even when she calls her family and me and her boyfriend all the time, it's not enough support," Jacklynn said.

"I feel guilty. I'm not lonely. I'm having a good—or at least an okay—time." Frequent crying notwithstanding.

She worried about Conner the most. They talked and texted daily, though their schedules were such that a text sent in the morning might not be returned until the late afternoon. Jacklynn went to bed before midnight and woke up early. Conner generally went to bed in the middle of the night and then slept until noon. The sweet spot was around 10:00 p.m. Central time, 11:00 p.m. Eastern, when they'd convene online for *Skribbl io* or *Minecraft*. Or do their schoolwork while on Skype. She was awed (and slightly horrified) by the amount of work he had. And how he somehow managed to get it done and still have time to check out clubs and events.

"I'm proud of him," she said. "His whole life, he's had to persevere through very tough obstacles." And though life at Columbia couldn't be easy, she knew he'd made the right choice. "I'm sure he's super excited to be where he is."

BRIANI

Spectator

On the day of the student activity fair, Briani headed into the drizzle and spent an hour squeezing through the crush of students, as club presidents hawked their mission statements and thrust flyers in her face. It was exciting—more than five hundred options. Briani signed up for the CU Democrats (Bernie all the way!), the Grupo Quisqueyano (Dominican Club), the Women of Color Pre-Law Society, the Multicultural Recruitment Committee, and Matriculate, a nonprofit that mentors high-achieving, low-income college hopefuls. She signed up for the CU Road Runners (but would drop out after nearly dying of exhaustion on the first run) and the Columbian Vegan Society. (She joined because her roommate, Brooklyn, was a vegan. She never actually attended a meeting.)

But really, Briani only had eyes for one club: the *Columbia Daily Spectator*, aka *Spec*, the student-run newspaper. She liked to imagine her byline in the paper—maybe even having her very own column.

To make *that* happen, she'd found her way to the Riverside Church on 122nd street for *Spec*'s info session. She'd been so excited that day, taking her seat among the other journalistic hopefuls, listening to the editors describe different sections of the newspaper. She was especially excited about *The Eye*, which published magazine-style features.

Briani believed deeply in the power of storytelling. Stories, she thought, could help people feel seen. It was why she'd signed on to a book project about her experience as a first-generation college student. Working as a student journalist was just another way to have that impact. And so she dreamed of diving headlong into a story, following sources for weeks, maybe even months. She wanted to see this campus and its students from the inside out. Wanted to spill the truth, send waves of it splashing down the brick and granite steps.

But the more the editors explained the application process and the new-staffer training program, the more uncertain she felt.

It was *a lot* of work.

It was *very* competitive.

It was a *huge* time commitment.

It was *supposed* to be only about eight hours a week, but Briani knew better. You didn't just stop reporting a story because some arbitrary timer buzzed. That wasn't how you got to the truth.

Spec did pay. It even counted toward work-study, the federal program that would help her fund the Student Responsibility. But it would leave her $600 short every semester.

This meant she'd need to pick up a second job, on top of whatever she was already doing for *Spec*, and the work she was doing for school, and the social life she was trying to jump-start.

Her parents had offered her some money. They didn't want

her worrying about a job her freshman year. But she wasn't going to take it. It wouldn't be right.

Which meant *Spec* wasn't possible, or practical, or wise.

It was disappointing, but being an adult meant making tough decisions. And she was an adult now. Like it or not.

BRIANI

Genevieve

As exhausting as orientation was, Briani was happy that she'd pushed herself. Yes, she was *that* girl in the elevator, cornering any warm body: *What's your name? Where are you from? I like your shoes.* She was on the lookout for anyone with a friendly, approachable vibe.

Genevieve lived in a single on her floor and ended up beside Briani at a dinner organized by their resident advisor. She was a Black woman, with a cloud of dark curls, a gliding model gait (because she'd modeled), and the self-possession of someone comfortable on the stage (because she was). She could have easily intimidated Briani. Instead, Briani saw warmth. She saw someone who was a little goofy, who could probably make a trash bag look stylish, and who had the guts to wear a jean skirt as a top. Definitely friend material.

John Jay had a dining hall on the ground floor. It resembled something out of Hogwarts: a lofty room of banquet-length tables, wood-paneled walls, and tall, Palladian-style windows. It was the kind of place that made you want to engage in "lively banter." So they did. Over mediocre pasta, Briani learned that Genevieve had grown up on Long Island but considered herself a Brooklynite—the eco-thrifting alterna kind as opposed to the hipster-beanie, skinny-jeans kind. With the help of Prep for Prep, a private school–access program for kids of color, Genevieve had gotten a scholarship from Saint Ann's School, an uber progressive, uber expensive independent institution in one of Brooklyn's wealthiest neighborhoods. Now she was covering Columbia through a combination of financial aid and some money her educator mom had put aside.

It was often uncomfortable to rely on other people's generosity when you didn't have much to give in return. She lived far from Saint Ann's and was constantly crashing at her friends' houses to avoid the long commute. She was frequently inside their brownstones but always a guest. Or as she explained, "You're in it and feel part of it. Then you go home and you're like, Oh, that's not my life."

Still, Genevieve had made good friends and excelled in high school. She built a stronger sense of self. Briani was impressed. And relieved. She'd never really crossed class boundaries before. Maybe with Genevieve's help, she could get through freshman year without falling on her face.

JACKLYNN

Think Positive

Jacklynn had one "blow-off class" called Navigating College. She knew this was about the college experience, but it still sounded silly to her; all her classes were in a single building. What was there to navigate? She was loving Intro to Sociology and Public Speaking. And hating on US History. She'd never been good at events and dates. Plus, she was a huge procrastinator. The night before her first exam, she set about memorizing four textbook chapters and sixty pages of handwritten notes. She crammed like no one had ever crammed before. The next morning, she drove to school thinking, *You know everything.* It was far from true. But you had to think positive. You had to will yourself toward success.

She furiously scribbled answers to essay questions and ended up guessing on five of the fifty multiple choice questions. She finished ten minutes early. Was that really good? Or really bad?

A few days later, her professor announced that grades would be posted online. When Jacklynn logged in that afternoon, there was nothing. A few hours later, she checked again. Still nothing. Then a few hours after that, she checked again.

Suddenly, there was her grade, sitting pretty like it had always existed, like it was a freaking prophecy. She'd gotten all five of her guessed questions wrong but had aced the other sections of the test. She had an A.

She hurried into the in-home office where her mom worked for a large insurance company. "Guess what!" she said, beaming.

Sherry was about as no-nonsense as they come. She was not a squealer. But she gave praise when it was due. "That's my girl," she said.

Jacklynn rushed out to Snapchat Conner the news. It wasn't the first college test she'd taken, nor the first college A she'd ever received. But it was the first time she'd received an A while being a full-time college student. She just hoped she could keep this up, for her scholarship of course, but also for her own pride.

BRIANI

Missing the Memo

About a week after the floor dinner her resident advisor organized, Briani texted Genevieve to hang out, and Genevieve said yes. It sounded small, but it felt significant. It was a victory and, as it turned out, one she really needed.

Because the night before their date, something happened. It was late, and Briani had returned to her dorm after some event. She was exhausted and wanted a hot shower and her head against the pillow ASAP. But so many doors on her floor were open. As Alberto said, this was how you made friends. She had to power through.

Her roommate, Brooklyn, a Black pre-med student from Upstate New York, agreed to hang and together they made the rounds, popping into one room, then another. At some point, the two of them ended up back in their own room chatting with a first year from another dorm and that girl's friends. Before long, the conversation shifted toward racial justice. This was a frequent topic of conversation on campus, and baked into everything, from the academic work to the identity-based clubs to the student government. That conscientiousness—that passion—was one of the reasons that Briani chose Columbia. But like many things in college, there was a learning curve.

In retrospect, the book project was bound to come up and, with it, questions about the white woman writing it. Was it Briani or Brooklyn who mentioned this? She couldn't remember. But this detail did not sit well with the girl from the other dorm.

"But that's exploitation," she said after Briani explained the project. "It's taking advantage of people who've had their own voices silenced, and it's going to further the agenda of people who haven't lived your experience."

The room had grown suddenly tense, like everyone was on high alert.

The girl continued, "It's not that I hate white people, but it's very easy for people of color to be used by white people. I don't want that to happen to you guys."

I'm just looking out for you. Briani was sure the girl had kind intentions. But deep inside she felt shook. It was like she'd been standing on dry land and then a second later, quicksand. Should she argue? What *could* she argue? She'd always considered herself to be both progressive and self-aware. Now, suddenly, she felt like the conservative in the room, the ignorant person who wasn't woke enough.

It hurt. She was used to being judged by conservatives and Trumpers, by well-intentioned but clueless Southerners. But to be judged by her own? The people she considered her allies? That turned everything upside down.

But what if the girl was right? *Did I miss the memo?* she wondered. *Is there something wrong with me? Am I letting people tokenize me and I don't know it? Am I really that naïve? Do I have to unlearn everything I've been taught?*

Briani felt the room closing in. She needed to get out of there.

But they were in *her* room! When the girl and her friends said they were heading to another dorm, Briani felt a wave of relief. She retreated to her bed and curled up on her speckled gray comforter. Here, among her Georgia-thrifted clothes and high school Polaroids, she'd created a nest for herself. A small island of comfort.

Growing up in Lawrenceville, she'd sometimes forget her key and get locked out of the house after school. Neither of her parents could leave their jobs to let her in, so she'd sit by herself on the curb and wait. Sometimes for hours. She knew how to be alone, how to rely on herself.

But just because she could didn't mean she wanted to. She just wanted to have a place here, people she could trust not to hurt her.

She missed her parents like phantom limbs.

She switched off the light, climbed under the covers, and cried.

BRIANI & GENEVIEVE

Choose Your Battles: Part 1

Briani woke up the next morning with the uncomfortable lump in her throat again.

That's exploitation.

She washed up, pulled on some clothes, grabbed her tote.

It's going to further the agenda of people who haven't lived your experience.

She met up with Genevieve and they walked across campus to Ferris Booth Commons dining hall on the third floor of the student center.

It's very easy for people of color to be used by white people.

They talked more about their backgrounds. Genevieve said her dad was a jazz musician who was mostly out of the picture and that she'd grown up in a three-bedroom suburban house with a large yard and a deck. Her mom had a master's degree from Teacher's College at Columbia. Which made Genevieve a legacy.

But she didn't *feel* like a legacy. Her high school classmates were the kids of actors and fashion designers. Many of them had second homes in the Hamptons and on Cape Cod. When they woke up in their multimillion-dollar Brooklyn Heights brownstones, they'd roll out of bed and be at school in five minutes flat. On the nights when Genevieve did not crash at one of these houses, she would catch the 7:17 a.m. train in from Long Island. She'd been making the trip by herself since age twelve.

She said she wanted to be an actor, but her mom preferred a more traditional path: Prep for Prep, followed by a prestigious high school, elite college, and a career with inherent earning potential. Stability and mobility.

Briani got it. José was less than thrilled about his daughter's love for journalism. He was eager to see her in law school. He'd recently contracted shingles and had no choice but to work every day, through the most excruciating pain. *It's like you want to rip your skin off with your mouth*, he'd told his daughter. A lawyer would have good health insurance. A lawyer would have sick days. Law appealed to Briani, which made José happy. But mostly public interest law, which did not.

The girls had been talking for some time, and the dining hall had mostly cleared out. Briani started to feel anxious. She was still thinking about last night. She was starting to ruminate. She wanted to talk about it, but could she? How would Genevieve react? She wasn't getting that combative vibe. In fact, Genevieve seemed to intuit that something was up.

"Are you okay?" she asked.

"I was crying last night," Briani said. And then the story spilled out: what the girl had said to her and how terrible it made her feel.

Genevieve listened, amazed that Briani already trusted her this much. Vulnerability was a gift, and when someone offered it to you, you treated it as something precious. *Her kindness and care*, Genevieve thought. *This is someone I really need and want in my life.*

She often felt like Saint Ann's encouraged kids to be individualistic to a fault, like they couldn't see the world beyond themselves. At times, they could be selfish and mean. Now that she was in college, Genevieve wanted to surround herself with people who were compassionate. People like Briani.

But like individualism, compassion could also be taken too far. She worried that Briani might drive herself crazy, trying to please everyone.

"Look," Genevieve said. "There's always going to be a conversation about who has the right to tell what stories. But it's not black and white. You shouldn't not do things because of what other people think."

"I know," Briani said. "I talked to my mom about that girl. She said I have to think for myself and question what other people say."

But Leonor was biased. She and José were conservatives. They worried progressive campuses like Columbia were shutting down free speech.

Briani didn't believe this was a liberal versus conservative situation. She just wanted to be able to trust herself. "What was it like for you being Black at your private school?" she asked Genevieve. "When people challenged you, how did you deal?"

Genevieve nodded as though to say, *Girl, do I have a story for you.*

Interlude: Genevieve's Story

Once upon a time, there was a woman named Love. When Love learned she was pregnant with a girl, she was filled with joy. So much joy, in fact, that she decided to call the baby Thandiwe. It was a Zulu name meaning *Beloved* in the South African language Nguni. Love and Beloved, a beautiful bond between mother and daughter.

But as Thandiwe grew up, she did not feel beautiful. She hated her color, hated her curly hair, hated her name.

In kindergarten one girl told another girl, "Don't play with Thandiwe, she's dark-skinned."

In elementary school, teachers apologized when taking attendance: "I'm sorry, I know I'm going to butcher this but, *Thand-wee*?"

On her very first day of Saint Ann's, a girl in her class said, "I saw your name in the directory, and my parents had a bet to see whether you'd be a girl or a boy."

One day, Thandiwe's English class was assigned *Song of Solomon*, by Toni Morrison. In the book, names weren't just symbolic; they were life defining. One day, a boy named Mike raised his hand. "I don't get why names are such a big deal," he said.

Without even thinking, Thandiwe went off.

"For some of us it is a big deal," she said. "We've had to go through so much to finally accept who we are and our names and where they come from. Maybe not for you, because your name is Mike, and there are a lot of Mikes in the world. You're also just a perfect-looking white guy with blond hair and blue eyes. Everything's perfect for you. But that's not reality for everyone."

Thandiwe heaved in her chair, angry and on the verge of tears. Everyone stared. Not even the teacher knew what to say. But after that, something shifted. She started to feel proud of her name. *Thandiwe* held all of her struggles and insecurities; it held her persistence as a young Black woman. If she could learn to love her name, she could love herself.

And yet.

When she started college, she decided to go by Genevieve, her middle name. Her reasoning was complicated. For one thing, her name was tied to a lot of negative experiences. It held baggage. Now she was starting fresh. Why couldn't she throw off some of the weight? But even more fundamentally, "I wanted to know what it feels like to come before my name," she said. "To meet my RA and the kids on my floor and not have everyone fixated on it."

Her mom respected all this, but she wasn't entirely comfortable with it. "I'm not calling you Genevieve," she said. On Instagram and Facebook, she started referring to her daughter as "Thandiwe Genevieve."

Over time, Genevieve came to see her given name as something sacred, a gift, to be given only at her discretion.

"Okay, Genevieve is nice, Genevieve's out there," she said. "Everyone can have a piece of her. But then I have this other part of myself that I save for people whom I truly care about."

Choose Your Battles: Part 2

Genevieve had learned something from blond-haired, blue-eyed Mike. "When people question you, you can be really mad and angry, or you can take the high road," she said. "Maybe ignorance is why they're acting this way, but I'm not going to dwell on that. Certain battles I'm not going to fight."

That resonated with Briani, who did not want to fight a battle for wokeness. "I'm not going to let anyone just change the way I think," she decided. "Because I knew—I knew what that girl said about exploitation wasn't right."

She also knew she had a lot to learn about inclusivity. Before applying to Columbia, she'd never heard the term *Latinx*, a gender-inclusive term for people with Latin American roots. She'd never given anyone her pronouns. There were so many things she'd never considered before—like the relationship between the story and the storyteller. So much of this was worth exploring. But exploring was not the same as judging.

Briani had grown up feeling judged. Like Genevieve, she often felt unbeautiful as a kid, lamented the traits she shared with her Mexican father: his broad cheekbones, indigenous nose, and small eyes. She longed for that Eurocentric beauty. In pre-calculus class her sophomore year of high school a kid told her that her lips weren't even "that nice" because they weren't "Kylie Jenner lips." That comment stuck with her for years. Perhaps she would have felt more confident if she'd been the "right" kind of brown. She used to wish her parents had called her Maria or Theresa. And her last name? Forget it. Almost nobody pronounced Netzahuatl right. Phonetically, it was *Natzwalt*. Its origin, Aztec. So she was at a double disadvantage: not your "normal" Southern American teenager and not your "normal" Latina. So many times she thought, "I'm not worth getting to know. I'm not that cool, and I just don't have a lot to offer."

She excelled in high school, but she knew she wasn't anyone's go-to image of an Ivy League student. She knew some people assumed Columbia only accepted her to boost its diversity profile. Briani believed in the Golden Rule: Do unto others as you would have them do unto you. She did not want to judge—at least not unless she had a reason. In the weeks to come, she would meet many people who jumped into judgment, sometimes for understandable reasons. And yet here was Genevieve, who wasn't judging, who looked at the world like she did: open-hearted and trusting and wanting to see the best in people. Was that a naïve way to see things? Briani didn't think so.

CONNER

SparkNotes

It was a few weeks into the semester, and things weren't going exactly as expected. It wasn't a big deal. His issues were really just hiccups.

Hiccup: The family had moved three times in the last year, which meant his mom couldn't find his birth certificate and Social Security card. Which, in turn, meant he couldn't get a work-study job to help cover his Student Responsibility.

Hiccup: His French class was too far away from his film class, which meant that he couldn't reasonably get to film on time. But his backup French class was likely full, so he'd been attending two different French classes (double hiccup?) while he waited for things to get sorted.

Hiccup: Literature and Humanities was not shaping up as expected.

"Lit Hum," as everybody called it, was a yearlong, mandatory freshman seminar held twice a week. According to the university website, the course gave students "the opportunity to engage in intensive study and discussion of some of the most significant texts of Western culture." Conner couldn't wait to dive into Homer and Montaigne and Woolf. He couldn't wait to bat around ideas and arguments with students who shared his passion for literature. On the very first day, though, he encountered not the free-flowing conversation he'd anticipated, but a bunch of kids jockeying to impress the professor with erudite (and, frankly, nonsensical) readings of *The Iliad*.

"I'd done the reading," he said. "But it was intense." He wanted to participate, but he couldn't imagine wading into the melee. Then, the following week, while walking to class with some kids from the seminar, he realized they were all cramming SparkNotes.

He was stunned. SparkNotes? At Columbia?

It was disappointing. But as always, Conner found a bright side. "The first day, I was disappointed from my lack of performance and not having prepared in advance," he said. As it turned out, his only fault was not having read the SparkNotes. "I'm using that to prop myself back up," he said. Moving forward, he wasn't going to worry about his classmates. He'd read for enjoyment and let the exploration happen between his brain and the page.

BRIANI

DWM

She was definitely nervous about Lit Hum. The course was a reminder that Columbia was literally not built for people like her. For instance, carved into the façade of Butler Library were eighteen names, seventeen of which were featured in the Core Curriculum, including:

Homer

Herodotus

Sophocles

Plato

Aristotle

Cicero

Vergil

If you aren't familiar with these names, they loosely translate to:

Dead White Male

Dead White Male

Dead White Male

Dead White Male

Dead White Male

Dead White Male

Briani knew this when she applied. It's partly *why* she applied. Familiarity with the Western canon would give her social access. She imagined engaging in high-minded philosophical debates, at fancy dinner parties, held in swanky New York City apartments.

Reality check: She was *not* getting invited to fancy dinner parties.

At least Columbia was trying to diversify! These days, Lit Hum included Virginia Woolf and Toni Morrison.

But it was hard not to be skeptical.

In high school, an older English teacher said Ralph Ellison's *Invisible Man* was about much more than race. Briani was flummoxed. Had the woman not lived through the civil rights movement? *In the South?*

"So for her, in her position, to say that a Black man writing about being *Black* doesn't think race is everything—at a time when the US literally had legal race separation—I just *knew* that wasn't right," Briani said. But from then on, she mostly kept quiet in class, afraid that pushing back might hurt her grade.

So she was a little shocked when her Lit Hum instructor, a female Hispanic cultural studies grad student, said, "This is a space to collaborate, to be active listeners, to not talk over each other. There are multiple interpretations to every text we're going to read this year."

The woman may as well have looked Briani in the eye and

said, *Your non-male, non-white, and very-much-living viewpoint is valid.*

For the first time in a long while, Briani walked away feeling that she could raise her hand.

CONNER

Anti-SparkNotes

The dining hall in John Jay may have looked "Ivy League," but it had the same disinfectant smell as Conner's high school lunchroom. Not that Conner minded. He was loving the grain bowls on offer, especially with baby corn and feta. He'd eat them with a side of scrambled eggs doused in ketchup and wash it all down with ginger ale.

He tended to visit the dining hall at off-hours. Sometimes, he'd just look for interesting people and sit down. On one particular afternoon, he emerged from the kitchen with his tray and spotted two guys debating Napoleon. They were so energized, Conner could hear them across the room. So he walked over and asked if he could sit down.

"Maybe if I'd known they were seniors, I would have been more intimidated," he said. Instead, all he saw were two friends having a rolling good time.

He set his tray on the table and nibbled his baby corn as their debate shifted from revolutionary theory to North Korean communism. Finally, at a pause, they asked who he was.

"I'm Conner," Conner said. "I'm a freshman."

"Yeah, we know that," one of the guys said. "Only a freshman would sit down like that and talk to us."

Conner wasn't sure what they were implying. Did they mean only a freshman would be confused enough or green enough or foolish enough to intrude on a couple of upperclassmen? Or maybe they meant only a freshman would have enough balls. No matter. He'd sat down, because this kind of spontaneous intellectual debate was precisely why he'd come to Columbia. He'd sat down because, out of the blue, he'd encountered the antithesis of SparkNotes, alive in the wild, just like he'd expected.

BRIANI

Imposter: Part 1

The day Briani got off the waitlist for International Politics, her professor said, "If you just got into this course and you haven't done the reading, you should drop. We've covered too much, and you can't catch up."

Briani gulped. She'd done *most* of the reading but not *all* the reading. How could she? The course packet was like a brick, the print so dark and compact every sentence could have weighed a pound. Back home, teachers frequently complimented her. Here, there was a distinct possibility they'd read her work and say, "Actually, you're trash and you can't write."

This pessimism wasn't good. Her coping mechanism, aka "stress starving," was worse. Her mom had been calling and texting daily: *Did you eat today? Call me and tell me what you ate.* (One day last week, the answer to this question was an apple and a yogurt.)

There was Just. So. Much. Work.

Her poli-sci professor talked really fast, but she didn't let students take pictures of the PowerPoint slides. So Briani recorded each lecture on her phone and then fully transcribed it back in her room. This was in addition to her furious, real-time note-taking.

Imposture syndrome was real. Yes, her Georgia public school

had a gifted program (which she was in) and a handful of APs (which she'd taken). It had even won a Great Schools College Success Award for two years running. But if seven out of ten white students were listed as "college ready," only six out of ten Black and Hispanic students received the same designation. The school had 2,660 students and, according to Briani, only one college advisor for five hundred seniors.

But her doubts weren't just about lack of preparedness. They were about lack of experience. Like on the first day of her International Politics section, the instructor asked each student to introduce themselves and say what they'd done that summer. Briani had volunteered at church camp and loved it. The girls had looked up to her, made her friendship bracelets. And yet . . .

"I went to Europe over the summer," someone said.

"I worked at a crisis shelter," the next person said.

"I volunteered for a political campaign," said a third.

Whoa. Briani was impressed but starting to feel a little . . . inadequate?

"I advocated for immigrants at the border," said a fourth.

Okay, what now?

Sure, her father had *crossed* the border, but being the daughter of a migrant was merely her existence, not a personal accomplishment. Doing super impressive, globally conscious humanitarian work during your summer break—that was an accomplishment. (Also, a privilege, given the money required for travel, housing, and food.) Not that these kids were trying to flex. Some of them actually seemed embarrassed by all the opportunities they enjoyed.

So they were aware . . . to a point. Because here's what Briani knew: to be embarrassed of your wealth was, itself, a privilege.

BRIANI

Imposter: Part 2

Walking out of section that day, Briani wondered what it would take to feel like a part of Columbia's culture—whatever that really meant. When would she wake up and simply feel deserving?

Of course she deserved to be here. But she kept questioning herself. Like Conner, she'd gotten to Columbia through Quest-Bridge, a college-access program for high-achieving kids whose families typically made less than $65,000 a year. If QuestBridge accepted you (itself an incredibly competitive feat), you could then apply to your top twelve schools early decision, ranked in order of preference. Then if of one of *them* accepted you (not a foregone conclusion), you'd get full financial aid to attend. Briani had worked her butt off to get into QuestBridge and then to get into Columbia. But not everybody saw this route as entirely legit. Briani knew it, so during senior year of high school, she'd hoped to keep her acceptance quiet—at least for a little while.

But her best friend, Maia, God bless her, took to Instagram with a grainy two-second video: Pan left to Briani's acceptance letter. Pan right to Briani in her Columbia sweatshirt, hiding her face from embarrassment. And below in all caps: MY BITCH IS GOING TO COLUMBIA Y'ALL.

The congratulatory messages poured in. We know how bad you wanted this, and we wanted this for you, her friends told her.

Then came another text: I'm proud of you girly. It was from Hanna, a former friend turned frenemy after Hanna had proclaimed her support for Trump.

"We need a leader who speaks his mind," she had told Briani.

"You know he hates me and my people," Briani had said.

"Look at Shakira," Hanna had said. "She's super famous." As though to say, *See, Hispanics aren't doing that bad.*

In any case, Briani doubted Hanna was actually happy for her, especially because the girl had just been rejected early from Harvard. Sure enough, the following week, Briani discovered Hanna had been talking out of school, saying Briani was lucky to have parents whose modest income paved the way for her Columbia acceptance. And by the way, if Briani's family was so poor, then why did she just get a new car?

For the love of God, enough with the car! Right before senior year, the family's ten-year-old Civic up and failed, and the mechanic said there was no point in fixing it. So José, who knew somebody at the dealership, purchased a used 2015 Toyota Corolla at a steep discount.

Briani texted Hanna: I did not receive a handout. And if you're mad at anybody, be mad at the system that makes us exploit ourselves and our struggles to get into school. I worked at my parents' business, at part-time jobs, stayed after school for hours, because my parents couldn't pick me up. You don't know everything about me. Please don't assume because I got a new car we are swimming in money.

Hanna replied that Briani was making her own assumptions. Just because her parents made six figures didn't mean they could easily afford a $200,000 liberal arts education.

Briani knew that Hanna had a point. She knew loans were a terrible option. Years before, José and Leonor had made it very clear that their children were not to borrow money for school. But without any kind of college fund, Briani was in a bind. College was the expectation, and she had no way to pay for it.

She didn't begrudge her parents for putting her in this catch-22. They merely wanted their kids to have the best shot at success. This meant funneling every dollar, every hour of the day, into creating a stable, middle-class existence for Briani and her younger brother, Joseph, even when their bank account suggested otherwise.

Needless to say, there were no tutors, no summer enrichment trips, no SAT prep courses or private college counselors. There was no weekly allowance for clothes and lattes and dinners out. So what *was* there? Well, love. Encouragement. Sacrifice. And, aside from a momentary freak-out over their daughter's senior prom date (he was just a friend!), there was complete trust. But with that trust came a massive responsibility: Briani's future was in her own hands. Hanna didn't—probably couldn't—understand what that was like.

On occasion, José would say, "Mija, I don't want you to be like me, working like a donkey for nothing. I hope you aren't embarrassed of me."

How did a person respond to that sort of selflessness? Embarrassed of him? She was awed by him. The only way to truly show it was to carry the weight of her future without complaint. She would do it, until she achieved everything her parents dreamed for her.

Eventually, Briani deleted Hanna's number and blocked her on Instagram. But the hurt persisted. In late February, she took to her finsta account for a postmortem. Luv when ppl with privilege STILL aren't satisfied even tho they have everything easier.

Rarely was she so harsh. But at a certain point, she couldn't keep the frustration bottled up. And everything worked out for Hanna in the end. She got a full ride to a highly respected, competitive college.

OCTOBER

CONNER

The Social Dorm

It was 2:00 a.m. on Saturday night and Conner was starving. He was awake, as he often was at that hour, working and chatting online with his Missouri friends. But he'd barely eaten all day. He considered his options. A few days ago, he'd swiped a package of S'mores Pop-Tarts from the dining hall. Then he'd come back from class one day to find them eaten, wrappers in the trash.

He asked his roommate, Omar, about it. Omar said he didn't know anything. He said someone must have come in the room when the door was open and eaten them.

Conner sent Jacklynn a photo of the wrappers in the trash can. She was angry. She wanted him to press the issue. But what would that accomplish? Omar was probably embarrassed. Conner didn't want to make things worse. He had to live with the guy, after all.

So there wasn't much on hand, and Conner didn't yet know that the junk food lair in the basement of John Jay Hall called JJ's Place stayed open all night.

Then inspiration struck: a pizza! He could eat the leftovers for days. And this was New York City. How could you *not* eat New York City pizza when you were hungry at 2:00 a.m.? Conner called in his order and went outside to wait for the delivery person.

He wasn't surprised to find a handful of kids on the dorm steps at this hour, but why were they lying on their backs, lolling around and laughing hysterically? Then he understood.

"It's starting to hit!" somebody shouted.

"It hasn't hit me yet. How long do I have to wait?"

"Does anyone know how long this is supposed to last?"

"Have you done this before? What's it going to be like?"

The delivery guy arrived. Awkwardly, Conner stepped around the prostrate bodies to retrieve his pizza. Then he stepped around them a second time on his way back up. "I should have known better than to go outside at 2:00 a.m.," he said.

Except this wasn't the only time. Wanting to do or doing hallucinogens seemed to be a frequent topic of conversation on campus. It was the same with edibles. And drinking. Man, was there a lot of drinking. Just last week, the suite adjacent to his own had thrown a rager: bass pounding through the walls until the RA eventually shut it down. Omar had also been having people over. A lot of people. Late at night.

As far as Conner could tell (since the lights were generally off), Omar's friends weren't drinking or doing drugs in the room. But they were definitely loaded when they arrived.

"I was kind of confused by how much partying there was," he said. "I've begun to accept it."

Conner didn't want to sound judgmental, but substances made him profoundly uncomfortable. His parents had both struggled with addiction; drugs had killed his dad.

His high school friends drank around him sometimes. But that was different, because with them the alcohol was incidental, like they'd be just as happy watching movies or grabbing burgers at Steak 'n Shake. Also, they knew Conner. They understood what he was dealing with.

The kids at Columbia were strangers. Omar was a stranger.

Of course to Omar, Conner probably seemed like a killjoy. He was so awkward when Omar had friends over. Or that one time, when Omar brought a girl to the room, Conner refused to just be cool and hang at the party next door for a couple hours.

But Omar didn't realize what he was really asking of Conner. Just as he didn't realize that eating Conner's food (and, according to Jacklynn, using Conner's shampoo) was a problem for someone who didn't have a lot of extra money to spend on snacks and toiletries.

Conner would never be completely free from the concerns of Missouri, but he'd looked at college as a kind of respite. A place where he could have some stability. Just a little more control over his surroundings. That was less true than he'd hoped.

Still, Conner wanted to make the best of things. He wanted to accommodate. Truth be told, he felt a little foolish. "I should have known what it meant that Carman was called the social dorm," he said.

He'd learned this phrase from a student message board and, based on that, had ranked Carman first on his housing list. "I assumed it would be social in the respect of, 'I'm going to Columbia and I want to meet people.' Not, 'I'm going to Columbia to party,'" he said. "I didn't expect people at an Ivy League school to be hitting it so hard."

The thing is, he couldn't even blame this misunderstanding

85

on being first-generation. Because Jacklynn, who was also first-gen, definitely got it.

"As soon as he told me he signed up for the 'social' dorm, I knew what that meant," she said. "If I'd known sooner, I would have shut that down."

BRIANI

Parents and Babies

Prior to orientation, Briani attended a four-day camping trip arranged by the school, her first-ever time wearing hiking boots or sleeping in a tent. The group leaders were upperclassmen, affectionately called "parents" to the freshmen "babies." And so it went that, early in the semester, the parents invited their babies to a mixer.

That sounded fun. Briani's friend Marsha was like, "What are you going to wear?"

And Briani was like, "Leggings and a T-shirt? It's just a mixer."

And Marsha was like, "Mixer means party."

And Briani was like, "Oh." Because she didn't go to parties in high school.

It wasn't her thing. She'd tried beer before, and it was gross. Also, her parents had fairly strict expectations and would not have been okay with that. But she was in college now and they didn't have to know.

The mixer, aka party, was in a suite on East Campus, aka EC, which was a bit of a trek from Briani's dorm. She and Marsha arrived around eleven. The suite was dark and cramped and smelled of beer. The music was a weird mix of Drake and the Killers. She said hi to her friends from the trip and decided to give the beer a try. She took the can from someone and lifted it to her lips. Reflexively, her tongue curled in disgust. *Still gross.* The room was getting crowded. Maybe if the music had been better . . . but *this is not it*, she thought. She looked at her watch. How long did she have to stay?

It was moments like these that she was relieved not to live in Carman. A girl she knew had seen kids doing lines in a bathroom there. Briani herself had watched people screaming and running down the hallways, possibly high. On weekend nights, the dorm's lobby was jam-packed with Barnard girls.

Someone yelled, "Okay, babies!" and Briani snapped back to the present. One of the parents was clutching a bag of wine, motioning for freshmen to line up and swig. That was her cue to leave. Maybe if there'd been room to dance, she would have stayed. But this wasn't worth missing sleep over.

So what was worth it?

Last Thursday night, hanging with Genevieve and their friend John, pretending to study for Frontiers of Science—aka Fro Sci, aka Fro Suffering. Or joking around after a floor dinner, while they all watched *Love Island*. Or taking a late-night run to JJ's in the basement of their dorm and stuffing their faces with french fries and pancakes. That's what she'd imagined college to be like.

BRIANI

Dominoes or How Not to Finish Your Lit Hum Homework

When one fell, they all did.

Domino: José's shingles weren't getting better, but no matter how much Leonor begged, he refused to rest. "He won't get better like this," she told Briani.

Domino: So Leonor picked up the slack. Usually, she took orders, managed the counter. Now she was waitressing, overseeing the kitchen, doing all the managerial work. Basically trying to run things from under her husband's nose to lighten his load. She worked harder and came home later, twice as tired.

Domino: Leonor's schoolwork fell by the wayside. For years, she'd deferred her own college dreams, worried that if she started on that path and failed, it would set a horrible example for her kids. Full-time work with benefits would show them what responsible adulthood looked like. In 2015, she decided to take the risk, though, and enrolled in an online bachelor's program at Liberty University. She'd been slowly advancing, a course here, a course there. She often asked Briani for help. But putting off high school assignments to help her mom write a paper was not the same as deferring college work.

Domino: Briani was not going to say no to her mom. "I can't be angry with her for asking," she said. "Maybe in the moment, I'm thinking, *I'm so tired, and I haven't even done my own work.* But if I was dealing with what my mom is, I'd put my work on the back burner, too."

Domino: Briani enlisted her cousin Alberto, and the two of them both pitched in to help with Leonor's psychology paper on behavior modification. It took a couple of days, and by the time the draft was complete, it was 11:00 p.m. the night before Lit Hum, and Briani hadn't started the reading.

Domino: She was totally unprepared in seminar the next day. But that was okay. In the end, one domino remained upright; Leonor was going to pass her class.

CONNER

Rage Cage

Conner loved Dr. John Pemberton, the hoary-haired professor who taught Intro to Social and Cultural Theory. Sure, the guy's voice creaked worse than the wooden floors, but his wrinkled smile exuded kindness and excitement. Exactly what you wanted in a teacher.

Conner loved how Pemberton's lectures wandered, like a dog that is constantly stopping to sniff at things on the sidewalk. *Oh, that nearly invisible hole in the ground looks interesting . . . oh, wait, is that the faint scent of squirrel urine?*

In early October, Pemberton was giving a labyrinthine lecture on an even more labyrinthine essay. He'd started with Franz Boas, wound around to Levi Strauss, done a three-point turn into Sigmund Freud, and then backed into Max Weber.

"Am I going too fast?" Pemberton asked somewhere in the middle of this speech. "I feel like I am. I had too much coffee this morning. I usually have one cup of oolong tea. How many people here drink coffee? How many drink tea? How many of you cook?"

Conner was picking up maybe 80 percent of what Pemberton said. Not too bad. In college, his professors routinely spent a single class exploring an idea that would have taken an entire semester in high school.

Now Pemberton said that in any community some people would prioritize their similarities with the group and some would prioritize their differences. For weeks, Conner had been trying to balance exactly this: fitting in and standing out. He was holding tightly to his identity. But it wasn't always clear if he was doing so by choice or because his FLI status put him in a box.

"Cultural norms are relative," Pemberton continued. "Do you know I ate dog twice? Once intentionally and once unintentionally."

This got everybody's attention. Except for Conner, who seemed to take the news in stride, like, *Of course Professor Pemberton has eaten dog and I'd be disappointed if he hadn't.*

Conner loved anthropology so much that he'd written his college application essay about it. His theme was "Nacirema," the idea that we're limited by our own worldview, especially when looking at other cultures.

Take the word *Nacirema.* It was actually a joke, but not one most people got right away. *Nacirema* is "American" spelled backward.

"Americans think the world totally revolves around them," Conner explained. "They don't even think to make fun of themselves." Case in point, in 1956, an essay titled "Body Ritual Among the Nacirema" had appeared in a serious anthropological publication without anyone being the wiser. Seeing *Nacirema* for what it was gave Conner an amazing rush.

It was a beautiful thing, he said, to realize what you don't know.

Which was why he eventually decided to further explore the Nacirema conventions of collegiate social life and go to a party.

It wasn't a frat party—there were some lines Conner was not going to cross, even in the name of research. Instead, it was a gathering of the Philolexian Society, aka Philo, the literary and debate club that Conner attended each Thursday night. Philo was officially founded in 1802, but claimed to have originated in the 1770s with Alexander Hamilton as a founding member. Meetings revolved around a single debate, absurd resolutions selected by the members.

Resolution: It Was *This* Big. (What was "it"? How big was "this"? Irrelevant.)

Resolution: City Slicker vs. Country Bumpkin. (Conner, being from Missouri, argued for Country Bumpkin. Missouri was, after all, the birthplace of Harry Truman.)

Resolution: You Can't Shit in the Same River Twice. (And to think that the kids debating this point had been high school valedictorians!)

Philo members were a particular brand of campus eccentrics: lovers of bad poetry, byzantine traditions, and strange artifacts (the club had a pepper shaker of particular importance). Anyone who attended a meeting, even if they wandered in by accident, was automatically a Philo member for life. Philo was simultaneously earnest and irreverent, much like Conner himself.

And yet after each Thursday night meeting, most of Philo headed off to East Campus, where the elevators smelled like piss or puke and nobody paid attention to fire codes. The club was emphatically egalitarian; even as a freshman, Conner was welcome to attend these parties. But so far, he'd begged off. It was a conundrum. To make friends *in* the club, you had to hang with them *outside* the club.

But could you really connect with people if everybody was hammered? It might have been one of their debates. Resolved: Sober or Smashed?

It was obvious which side would win. Even so, Conner decided to take the risk. Country Bumpkin had just prevailed over City Slicker (in large part due to Conner's efforts), and he was feeling good. Also, someone said there wasn't a lot of money to buy beer that week, so Conner assumed the party would be fairly dry.

It was not.

He waded into a sea of Solo cups bobbing in the half-dark. Why, he wondered for the millionth time, did people not want to see who they were talking to?

Someone set up a game of Rage Cage. It involved chugging beer, bouncing Ping-Pong balls into the empty cup as quickly as possible, stacking the cups, and then passing them around the table. The losing player passed their stack, picked a new cup, and drank. If your ball went into a filled cup, you drank. The game didn't end until all twenty or thirty cups of beer had been consumed. Conner asked if he could play without drinking, and Anderson, an elected Philo official, offered to be his surrogate. As it turned out, Conner was excellent at Rage Cage, but maybe that's because he was the only person to start off entirely sober.

Nobody seemed to care. Nobody pressured him. But the alcohol consumption was crazy. People were drinking while playing drinking games, which seemed like a terrible strategy. After setting up a game of beer pong, someone said, "I'll grab the stones," and Conner wondered if they were putting stones in the cups to steady them. Then he realized they meant Keystone beer. He watched with amazement as four kids, including Anderson and a huge Slavic guy named Misha, polished off a 24-pack. Beer pong went into triple overtime.

Later, Conner said that he might have skipped the party, had he realized the lack of beer money had no real impact on the amount of beer. But he was grateful for the experience. He'd learned some things. Like how drinking games worked. And what everybody did after Phllo each Thursday. In short, he knew what he was missing. He wouldn't have called it beautiful. But it was valuable nonetheless.

JACKLYNN & CONNER

A World of Their Own

Jacklynn was obsessed with digging holes. It wasn't exactly what Conner had in mind when he got them a *Minecraft* account. He'd done it to give them a long-distance project and because he knew Jacklynn would love world-building. He wasn't wrong. During the many hours they spent playing together, they'd fashioned an adorable farmhouse beside a thriving farm.

But pastoral Eden, this was not.

Minecraft offered two traditional modes: Creative and Survival. Jacklynn preferred Survival mode, where you had to scavenge, hunt, and fight for resources. Nothing had ever been handed to her, and the digital world was no different.

But she was ruthless. She'd tear down, like, six villages and commandeer all the resources. Conner was a little horrified. He'd expected this to be wholesome fun. "One of the first things she does is beat a sheep to death," he said. "Okay, you have to get wool from the sheep to make the bed, but she kills every animal she sees."

Jacklynn was just being practical. "We have a house now, don't we?" she asked him. *We have food, clothes, blankets, fortifications.* But it was more than that. She wanted to expand the world past its limits. No mill in the game? She'd build one. No ocelots roaming the countryside? They'd travel to the jungle and lure them back. (It wasn't easy; the ocelots put up a fight. But later, when their chicken situation got out of hand, Jacklynn just let them loose in the chicken coop. Problem solved.)

She was also excavating the earth under their house. She dug a mine with connecting tunnels, plowed deeper and deeper, because why not? Conner found this monotonous. Jacklynn found it meditative. Sometimes, if she'd had a bad day at work or was feeling anxious, she'd hunt some zombies. Instant catharsis.

Jacklynn and Conner were thusly engaged one evening after a long shift for Jacklynn at Big Whiskey's. The job could be exhausting even on slow nights. Among her responsibilities: serving, hosting, and expo-ing—making sure every dish had the correct sauces and garnishes. A small slipup could ruin her mood. Like if somebody said no tomatoes, but the plate came out of the kitchen with tomatoes, and Jacklynn failed to intervene, the customer could get snippety with the server or leave a lousy tip, which would then make the server angry at Jacklynn, even though it wasn't really her fault. At least in the world she'd created with Conner, she had total control.

Since he generally played at his dorm-room desk, Conner didn't have the same privilege. After midnight, as they were expanding their pigpen, Jacklynn watched Conner get up and disappear from view. When he returned, he reported that some kids were looking for his roommate, saying Omar had invited them to hang. Conner said he didn't know where Omar was.

Ten minutes later, Jacklynn saw Omar arrive and ask if he could have a few people over. Conner said sure. He was trying to be a good sport. And probably, Conner told her, it would just be some kids from the hall. It was one in the morning on a Thursday, after all.

Soon, though, the room had filled up. Then someone shut off the lights, plunging Conner into near darkness. Music came on and, with it, singing. Loud singing that was almost like shouting.

This was not a hang out. This was a party.

"Conner!" Jacklynn said, trying not to yell. Her mom was asleep in the other room.

"I can't hear you!" Conner shouted back.

Over Skype, she watched his face flicker in the glow of Christmas lights Omar had hung over his bed. She watched the butts and hips and backs of Omar's friends press around Conner's chair and desk. She felt like they were squeezing her, too, like these strangers had invaded her bedroom. She was starting to get a headache and turned down the volume on her computer. But then she couldn't hear Conner.

Honestly, she didn't know where to direct her frustration. At Omar, of course, but also at Conner. She wished he wasn't so accommodating. After the Pop-Tarts incident and the shampoo pilfering, she encouraged Conner to say something. *Talk to him about boundaries. Or try to switch rooms.* "This is making you miserable," she said. But Conner wasn't about confrontation. He didn't think switching rooms was possible.

Conner was reaching his limit, though. He considered texting the RA, asking him to say some other room had made a noise complaint. On the other hand, Omar's friends were plenty nice. A while back one of them had even walked a heavily intoxicated Omar back to the room and sat with him in case he puked. And it's not like Conner *never* talked to them. He *could* say goodnight to Jacklynn and hang out. He just didn't *want* to. He wanted to talk to Jacklynn, his girlfriend, who treated him like he existed.

But in some ways, he didn't exist. He was in the digital ether, floating between Manhattan and Ozark. In some ways, he was so removed from his current reality that he'd started building a new one.

"I don't think he's adjusting well," Jacklynn said a few days later. "I don't think he's happy. It breaks my heart. I think his world has been so rocked by the whole change that it's hard to reestablish what he had here."

It was 3:00 a.m. Eastern time, 2:00 a.m. Central, before Omar's friends finally left. Jacklynn noticed that some of them even told Conner goodbye by name. "I guess they knew each other?" she said. But this didn't make her feel any better. "The fact that we can build this world together means something to us," she said.

For his part, Conner had not moved to New York to recreate Missouri. And maybe he was spending too much time on the phone with his mother, assuaging her fears, managing her anxieties. He did the same for Ayden and Jacklynn. But if his mother, his brother, and his girlfriend needed a lot from him, their love for him equaled if not exceeded their needs. Which meant he never seriously considered hanging up with Jacklynn to join Omar's party. "It wasn't for me," was how he summed up the night. And at least Omar's friends never sat on his bed without asking first.

A few days later, Omar called Conner and asked to bring ten people over. Conner was online with his friends. He decided to channel a little bit of Jacklynn. *Boundaries*.

"You can if there's really nowhere else, but aren't the lobbies open?" he said.

"What, are you too busy playing *Minecraft*?" Omar scoffed and hung up. Conner didn't see him for the rest of the night.

BRIANI

Streetlights, Big Dreams, All Lookin' Pretty

It was Indigenous Peoples Day weekend, known in less progressive circles as Columbus Day, and her good friend Maria was flying in. Maria, a sophomore at the University of Georgia, whose face flickered from kind to sassy in a single smile. Her arrival felt like a reward. Briani had made it to the middle of the semester with (nearly) all her midterms complete.

They celebrated with a rare night of abandon, a movie montage of locations across Manhattan, set to the soundtrack of their laughter.

They grabbed Shake Shack for the world's latest lunch, then hurried into their finest:

Briani in a wine-red tiered sheath with a plunging V-neck, oversized white jean jacket, and Reeboks.

Maria in a floor-length trench coat over red and white polka dots, her thick hair flying wild.

Genevieve in a tan miniskirt with a dangerous side slit, silver go-go boots, and a faux-fur coat.

Then a swipe of red lip for Briani and Maria, and they were out the door.

Briani was excited to introduce Maria to Genevieve. She was pretty sure the collision of these worlds would produce a beautiful explosion. But Genevieve wasn't sure. Briani and Maria had grown up in the same neighborhood. Briani had only known Genevieve a few short months. Genevieve worried she'd feel like an outsider. She worried that Briani would compare her to Maria and realize they didn't have much chemistry at all.

The plan was to have a photoshoot on the Met rooftop—their student IDs got them in for free—but they arrived to find the roof closed for a private party. Suddenly, they were all dressed up with nowhere to go. So they did the only possible thing and plunged into the city.

There was vegan ice cream in lieu of dinner, followed by a jaunt through Central Park, where they stumbled on Bethesda Fountain (Briani recognized it from *Law & Order*) and mugged for Instagram in the echoing portico. Briani shot video of Maria and Genevieve leaping not-quite-balletically under the arches. They wanted to pose, but Briani was laughing too hard.

"Think of something sad!" Maria ordered once she'd taken over control of the camera. "Think of your GPA!" Which only made Briani double over in laughter.

They walked past the iconic Dakota apartment building, where John Lennon lived and was killed, twenty-one years before Briani was born. They practiced strutting down the avenues and across side streets, Maria trying to get the shot for her vlog without a car running them over. Genevieve had a perfect model walk and a cool wink. Briani tried to emulate her friend, but admitted she was basically walking like a normal person. It was silly and wonderful but meaningful, too. Briani looked at her beautiful friends, saw their heads held to the sky, felt the warmth of their pride. She was no different from them. She was also beautiful and confident. Could it be that she was only just starting to realize this?

They returned to campus at a wonderfully unreasonable hour. Briani jumped in the shower and when she emerged, she heard squealing in the hall. *Kids being loud*, she thought. Only it was Maria Roller Derby-ing it up and down the hallway in Genevieve's roller skates. Some guys came out of their room annoyed, asked what was going on, and returned to studying. For the first time, Briani and her friends were the ones making too much noise.

It thrilled Briani to see her friends having so much fun. And Genevieve realized she'd been worried about nothing. In fact, when she stopped to think about it, it seemed that her relationship with Briani had accelerated over the course of the evening. By 2:00 a.m., when the trio headed downstairs for a late-night snack at JJ's, it was like they'd known one another forever.

"All my friends at NYU feel like they don't have to do any work," Genevieve said, as the girls huddled around their Beyond Burgers and french fries. They were still riding high from the night, wishing it weren't such a unicorn event. "They're always going out, seeing the city. And we're like, Dang, we're studying every weekend."

"Not all of us," Briani pointed out. "Like all those kids on the floor who spent last week kiki-ing around. Do y'all not have tests? Maybe they feel entitled. Maybe their parents bought a building!" She was kidding, not kidding.

Genevieve nodded. "It's those kids whose style is 'rich,'" she said. "You're not putting together an outfit. But more like, 'This cost three grand, so let me wear it with whatever.'"

Earlier that day, Briani and Maria had seen two girls leaving the dorm with matching Louis Vuitton suitcases. "Which are already expensive," Briani said, "but these were monogrammed. And her friend had Yeezys on. I try not to judge." She paused. The friends chewed in silence for a moment. "She was *so* rich!" Briani burst out.

Maria started cracking up, which made Briani laugh. "Her blown-out hair," Maria said, wiping tears from her eyes. "Like first class!"

"That bag is, like, ugly cute," Briani said. "Rich people know ugly cute."

The girls tallied up their night. A couple of train rides, Shake Shack, and ice cream. The whole outing had cost each of them about $20. That was one dollar more than Genevieve made an hour at the bougie lounge where she worked as a hostess.

"Nineteen dollars an hour?" Maria couldn't believe it. "I was a hostess in Georgia and I got paid like nine dollars an hour. Now I'm the front-desk manager at a Massage Envy and I get eleven."

"It's next door to Le Bain at the Standard," Genevieve said. "You've heard of it. It's where Solange snubbed Jay-Z."

The girls gaped. Coming from anyone else, this might have made them roll their eyes. But Genevieve had this way of being both glam and totally real. Unlike the ugly-cute girls. Or the kids Briani had heard in the elevator last week. "These people were trash-talking Columbia," she said. "Saying Harvard, Yale, and Princeton are so much better and nicer. That Columbia isn't even a big, *big* Ivy."

The girls agreed that no school was perfect, but when you considered how many people would kill to be here . . .

"Did you say anything?" Maria asked.

"I wanted to," Briani said. "It sounded so ungrateful." But to butt in like that wasn't really her thing. And what would it accomplish?

"I thought because I'm still in New York, I'd know what people here would be like," Genevieve said. "But there are still messy people here. People without good intentions. I was put off guard by that." She was thinking, *I may look confident and outgoing, but most of the time I don't feel that way.* She said, "Some of the people here might come from small towns where they never encountered someone with a different skin color. What if I'm seen in a negative light because they don't understand what's different from them?"

Briani and Maria empathized. They were from Georgia. Being brown women in the South, in the Trump era, wasn't easy at all.

BRIANI

Big Apple Church

No way they were making it to church on time. The weather was brutal and they needed about ten more hours of sleep. The morning had started off almost balmy, but by the time Briani and Maria emerged from the subway at Times Square—all grit and concrete grayness—the rain was driving at them like it had a personal vendetta. Somehow, it felt wetter and colder here than it did on campus. The girls longed for a soft place to nestle. They'd have to make due with spiritual solace.

Briani attended church almost every Sunday, either here or in the Bronx with her aunt. On Wednesday nights, homework permitting, she went to a second service in Greenwich Village run by the International Churches of Christ. In Georgia, if you missed a service, people noticed, and they made sure you knew it. Here, thankfully, they seemed to care more about the effort than perfect attendance.

The Sunday service was held in an auditorium on 41st Street. By the time the girls arrived, the service was already underway, organ music echoing through the lobby. They passed a projection of the church logo—red apple, with a heart at its core—and made their way past rows of red-velvet seats toward the stage. They found seats in the second row among the other college students.

Hallelujah, your love makes me sing!

The singer was a portly white man with a steel wool beard and a sport coat. Briani began to sing along, though with less of an exclamation point in her voice. She was still trying to get warm. She opened a Bible app on her phone.

The singing ended, and the old white man was replaced by a young white man. He looked like Andy Samberg from *Saturday Night Live*: a handsome goof with a bouffant of brown hair. At first, he was lighthearted, cracking jokes as he related a teenage mishap. As a kid, he said, he'd broken his neighbor's window with a soccer ball. "I ran away. I thought it was no big deal. Nobody will know." Andy Samberg looked directly at the audience. "But I knew."

He said the guilt nagged at him.

Then he turned serious. "The world is a moral sinkhole," he said. "Money, sex, and power. But what amount of money can guarantee our future? There is no number."

Briani was taking notes in her prayer journal. Did she really buy this? Because look at José, working himself sick at the family business. Look at the wealth on display at Columbia. Look at Aunt Becky. Look at all those kids who could afford the private schools and tutors and summer service trips and vacations. *Well, money can't provide a spiritual future. But future in this world? Definitely.*

"Real power isn't using economic or educational privilege to get our way," Pastor Samberg continued. "It's abuse, false confidence, fear of being exposed. The false power of selfish ambition."

Now *that* Briani could get behind. That made sense.

Communion came around, baskets of small capsules that

looked like Japanese jelly candies. Briani and Maria each took one, pulled back the cellophane, and drank down the juice. They bowed their heads in prayer. A band took the stage and the service came to an end with a rousing soul number. *Oh God, hear my call. Lift me up so I can sing your praise!*

BRIANI & MARIA

Sunday Brunch

After church, the girls walked through the drizzle to a Hell's Kitchen diner, laughing about whether Briani should be a VSCO girl for Halloween—or whether she already was one.

"Checkered Vans and Fjällräven backpack?" Maria asked.

"Both thrifted!" Briani countered.

"Stack of friendship bracelets?"

"My campers at church camp made them for me!"

"Scrunchie on the wrist?"

"Okay, I have no excuse for that."

"Sticker-covered water bottle?" Maria frowned.

"Yeah, but it's not a pricey Hydro Flask."

They stood in line outside the diner, pressing against the window to avoid the rain. They were talking about midterms and how much work they still had. What the pastor had said about ambition—Briani felt that. "In high school, I was working so hard to get into Columbia," she said. "Now I'm thinking that my grades have to be really good so I can get into law school." She was starting to lament the Columbia Core big-time. "Can you imagine not getting into law school because of Frontiers of Science?"

She said the professor allowed a single cheat sheet, which she'd crammed with formulas so small you needed a microscope to read them. She said a bunch of kids on her floor seemed to be taking the test far less seriously. "They're all kiki-ing around. It's like do y'all not have tests?"

It was like those kids in the elevator, those kids with the Louis Vuitton everything. You couldn't imagine those kids huddled against the rain outside a random diner on 9th Avenue.

Fifteen minutes later, the girls slid into a booth and opened their menus. They were the size of Ten Commandments tablets and biblically complex, but with pictures. Maria settled on pancakes with scrambled eggs and sausage. Briani ordered pancakes with bacon. She wanted real maple syrup, but it cost $1.75 extra.

Briani said that she was constantly reminding herself to walk through life like Jesus: with humility, generosity, and kindness. "Even in some churches it's us versus them," she said. "But we're all God's people. Jesus didn't *other* people."

She worried that she othered wealthy people. You could have money and be unhappy for any number of reasons. Still, it was hard to look at wealth and not feel the lack of it in your own life.

Maria agreed. She'd recently transferred to the University of Georgia from community college and catered at Sanford Stadium. "Those suites are like two hundred thousand dollars a year," she said. "Everyone in there is a CEO or a doctor. Their wives are so pretty and their kids are all in designer clothes." She said it was awkward waiting on fellow students. Last week one of the suite owners was out of town and let his son use the place. "All these kids showed up. They went crazy around the room, drank all the alcohol, and threw food everywhere. And then after the game ended, they wouldn't leave. It was a disaster to clean up."

Maria said the owners themselves didn't act that way. In fact, the owner's son was really apologetic and even helped them clean. But Maria didn't get tipped. "Oh," she said. "And the governor goes there often. He's so problematic."

She was referring to Brian Kemp, who'd been a close ally of President Trump and had run on a staunchly conservative, anti-immigrant platform. In one campaign video, he boasts about using his "big truck" to "round up criminal illegals." He revs the engine. "Yep," he says with a smirk. "I just said that."

In 2018, Kemp won the governorship with 50.2 percent of the vote. He beat out Stacey Abrams, who would have been the state's first Black, female governor. And sure, Georgia had not elected a Democrat in twenty years, but Briani and Maria were kind of terrified to see Kemp ascend to the state's highest elected office. To think that half of Georgia's population voted for him! They'd done so either in spite of his anti-immigrant views (which meant they didn't care) or because of them (which meant they were racist).

Briani asked Maria if she'd ever put pepper in Kemp's drink.

"You just smile and keep going because that's your job," Maria said. But it didn't feel good. Maria was an asylum seeker from Colombia who had entered the country illegally with her family. And if Kemp had known—what then? He sat there in the plush comfort of his expensive box, watching football and making jokes about deporting people like the young woman serving his drink.

Maria said her family's asylum claim had been accepted; in

fact, she'd just become a citizen a few months before. But things were rough. Entering the country illegally—even if you were fleeing war, terrorism, or gang violence—can lead to criminal charges. And for some reason, despite her receiving citizenship, her mother's charges remained on her record. "She tried to get a job teaching at my school, but she couldn't," Maria said.

She barely choked out the statement, though, because suddenly, she was crying, her head bowed over the remains of her breakfast.

"The kids at the border right now in the cages"—she swallowed—"that really messes me up. That really easily could be me. They came seeking asylum, which is the same thing I did."

Maria was crying harder now. Briani touched her shoulder. There was something building behind her eyes: a scream, a growl maybe. Maria's shoulders shook.

"They separated my dad and put him in a camp, which was like a prison. They didn't separate me from my mom, because we were little kids. But the kids now are in cages by themselves. There's no one taking care of them. "It's literally"—she gulped for air—"it's the same way I got here . . ."

Briani's face had softened. Her anger had given way to tears. Her head was bowed as though in prayer.

"You come trying to survive," Maria said. "You become part of this country, and then they don't want you here."

Briani hugged her friend. Around them, the diner din continued: the clink of silverware, the clatter of plates. Brunchers talking over omelets and coffee. It was so easy for most people to ignore these things—the children at the border and the heartless man who put them there.

Briani looked up. "My parents . . ." She started to speak and then broke down. "Support him."

She didn't mean Kemp. She meant Donald Trump.

"I tell my dad, 'He literally does not care about you at all. He doesn't see you as who you are. He doesn't see where you come from as a place worthy to be recognized.'" Her voice had grown hard.

Leonor and José owned a small business and believed Trump was good for small-business owners. Briani countered that Trump was a failed businessman and irredeemably corrupt. Her parents didn't seem to care.

Or, she wondered, was this how to belong? Did you join the MAGA parade because maybe, if you were among the shouting masses, you couldn't hear that people were shouting about you?

The busboy began clearing their plates. He looked to be from Mexico or Central America and could have easily been undocumented himself. About 36 percent of workers without papers in the city were hired by the restaurant industry. In fact, this was just the kind of diner where José worked after he arrived in New York.

Briani did not miss a beat. She thanked the busboy for taking their plates. Then she said, "When you wear a MAGA hat, even if you don't think that's wrong, I already think you don't see me as a person. That's one reason I wanted to leave the South so badly." She'd stopped crying. "I was one of the few people of color in my high school class," she continued. "And you become a spokesperson for your race: the one Latina girl. When kids say terrible things, are you going to say something? It takes a toll on you. It adds up over time."

"We are first-generation Americans," Maria said. "The first in our families to go to college in the States."

"But they don't recognize what you can bring to this country, that you have something to give," Briani protested. "You feel like you have to work so hard in school and be the best because there's no plan B. When I was in the elevator with those kids . . ." New tears balanced in the corners of her eyes. "I try not to be mad at them . . ." Her lips quivered, as though she knew she would not win this battle in her heart. Why was it so hard to see the world through Jesus's eyes? "If they didn't want to be here, why would they come here? If they were going to be selfish and ungrateful, why did they come?" She shut her eyes and the tears spilled over.

The girls wiped their tears and sat in silence. The diner had nearly cleared out. The room had a skeletal look: scattered chairs and crumpled napkins.

Briani took a deep breath, gathered herself. "You need to get these things out," she said. "It's so heavy. It will literally sit on your chest."

NOVEMBER

CONNER

The Phone Call

It was 4:00 a.m., though Conner didn't remember the exact day. If it was Saturday, he was playing games with his friends in Missouri. If it was Sunday, he was studying. But he was awake. Which meant when his mom called, he was spared that dreadful moment of anxious confusion: *Where am I? What's happening? Is everything okay?* Instead, it was just the anxiety: *Something's wrong.*

"Mom?" Conner asked.

"Are you on Adderall?" Stacey demanded. "The school called and said you were on Adderall."

Conner looked over at Omar's sleeping figure. Could he hear any of this? Stacey sounded frantic.

"I'm not on Adderall," Conner said.

"What about acid, cocaine, heroin?" she continued. "Meth, marijuana. The school called. They told me."

Right now, the only thing coursing through Conner's body was frustration. Conner knew she was paranoid, even hallucinating. But how could she question his sobriety? It hurt, to hear these accusations from his mother. Because when Stacey was lucid, she knew him. She trusted him completely.

"Mom, I'm fine. I'm not on drugs."

"The school called; they said you're on drugs."

How many times did they go around like this? Her questions, his reassurances. Eventually, Stacey said she was going to sleep, so Conner did, too. Should he have been more concerned? He did not think to call anyone back home. His mom had her moments, and this was a moment. It was certainly not the first call of its kind since he'd been away at school.

The next day, though, he learned that Stacey was in the psychiatric ward. Conner wasn't the only person she'd called last night. She'd also rung up her father and accused him of giving Ayden AIDS. His grandfather alerted Stacey's sister, who found a cousin to stay with Ayden, while she took Stacey to the hospital. Things hadn't been this bad since late summer, when his mom's thirteen years of sobriety (temporarily) ended.

But how could he have known how bad things were? He'd become used to these late-night calls, as horrible as that sounded. Even Jacklynn wasn't shocked by it anymore.

A few days later, Stacey was back home with new medication. And Conner could tell that she was trying hard: cooking dinner for herself and Ayden, assuring Conner she would eat more, because she was pretty underweight, giving Ayden a bunch of his birthday presents early. Conner said she looked all right on FaceTime, like maybe the new meds were working. But it was hard to know.

JACKLYNN

The Friend Request

Jacklynn and her mom still had a landline with an old-school answering machine. That, unfortunately, set the whole thing off. It was Friday morning, November 1st, and Sherry pressed play just as Jacklynn was heading to her shift at Big Whiskey's. The voice she heard was male, deep with a light southern twang, at once foreign and familiar. She froze.

The voice belonged to Kelly, her father.

Jacklynn had not heard from her father in five years.

Now his voice was invading their home, saying he wanted to talk to them, to apologize.

Jacklynn could barely process this. She did not want to hear her father, let alone hear *from* her father. She had work. She had school. She had an especially difficult history paper due on Monday. She ran out the door so she wouldn't be late.

But by the time Jacklynn arrived at the restaurant, she had a series of texts from her sister Crystal saying their dad had gotten himself a Facebook account. *I wanted to tell you in person*, Crystal texted, *but I didn't know when I'd see you.* Jacklynn pulled up Facebook and sure enough, her father had sent her a friend request.

It seemed trivial.

It wasn't trivial.

Her father was an alcoholic. When Jacklynn was fourteen, her mother decided she'd had enough verbal abuse, enough fighting, enough uncertainty. After two decades of marriage, Sherry kicked him out. Since then, Jacklynn had only heard snippets about his life from Crystal: that he was intermittently homeless, that he bounced between shelters, that he couldn't or wouldn't hold down a job, that he was in and out of jail for DUIs. He'd told Crystal that he'd been sober for most of the year, though Jacklynn wasn't sure she believed it. At one point, a letter addressed to her dad—possibly a ticket or court summons—had arrived at their house. Sherry held the letter up to the light and was able to make out words like *trespassing*, *public nudity*, and *public urination*.

Jacklynn sent a group chat to her friends: Guess whose dad decided to contact her after five years? She was making light, but underneath, pure panic. She and her mother had spent five years building a cocoon of support and stability, a loving home just for them. Her dad had no right to barge in now.

Jacklynn was at the hostess station that day, and fortunately there weren't any customers in line. She was crying now, just full-on bawling. She was angry and embarrassed. She rushed out to the parking lot. Sobbing, she called her mom: "What do I do?"

"He sent me a friend request, too," Sherry said. "It's your choice, but if you accept it, you'll most likely end up getting hurt."

But this was her dad. Shouldn't she at least be able to keep track of him, to know if he was alive or dead? And she felt bad. Was she going to be the daughter who rejected her father's friend request?

She pressed accept, drank a Red Bull, returned to her shift. But she couldn't focus. She was no use to anybody here. So Jacklynn went home. Luckily, the general manager was her cousin and wouldn't get her in trouble for leaving early.

JACKLYNN

Facebook Photo

Midterms waited for no woman. The events of your personal life were irrelevant. The test was scheduled and the paper was due, and if you didn't get it done, you failed. Maybe in high school Jacklynn could have talked to her teacher and gotten an extension. But this was college, and making excuses wasn't something she'd feel good about doing.

And so, she had two days to complete a four-page, four-source research paper about a major historical event between 1865 and the present. As usual, she'd waited until the last minute. In high school, she'd been able to get away with that. In college, not so much. She'd never been good at history, but this was also the first time she'd been asked to find the sources and craft the argument entirely on her own.

Now she had a folder of thirty sources about women in the workforce during WWII. She had no idea how she was going to organize this information, let alone develop a cogent argument. In just two days. And with this dad drama.

The stress of the paper did not make her forget the stress of her father.

She pulled up Facebook, pulled up his profile.

Hold on.

She was looking at herself—a photo snagged from her own Facebook page and reposted. She was serene in the picture, sunlight dappled across her face. It was like her dad was trying to show her off, pretend that he deserved some credit for her smile.

She felt sick inside.

CONNER

Board Game Club

Officially, it was called Games Club and, according to the Columbia website, offered students the chance to play "board games, war games, role-playing games, head games, games of chance, games of strategy and games of cunning."

Conner was up for most of these. He looked forward to the club all week. Here, finally, was a social event with other like-minded people and *without* substances. On this night in November, Conner was in the middle of a complicated civilization-building game called Terraforming Mars, which involved tiny plastic cubes, playing cards, and clip art. He was just starting to make some headway building a space station, when Jacklynn started blowing up his phone. Something was seriously wrong. He folded his cards, apologized to the others. *I have to go. My girlfriend . . .*

In fact, he'd had plans for the whole night. He was considering going to a second Philo party later on. But no matter, Jacklynn needed him. He hurried back to his dorm.

"I'm so sorry," she said as soon as he Skyped her. "I didn't want to make you leave. But I don't know what to do." She told him about the phone call and the friend request. She didn't have to explain about her dad or how all this made her feel. He already knew. Over the last two years, they'd spent so much time talking about their families. They'd seen each other through the craziness. And neither the craziness nor the witnessing of it was going to stop just because they were in college.

"Do you want to block him?" Conner asked. "If you don't block him, he might think it's okay for him to talk to you."

"I know," Jacklynn said. "I'd thought about that, too."

She felt better, just knowing they were on the same page. They continued talking late into the night until she couldn't stay awake any longer. Conner looked at the time. Board Game Club was definitely over by now. He wondered if the Philo party was still happening. Possibly. He could have texted someone to find out, but he didn't really feel like going anymore. You had to be in the right brain space for that kind of thing. Instead, he played some video games and went to bed.

JACKLYNN

Aftermath

The second she opened her eyes on Sunday morning, panic flooded in.

She pulled up her dad's Facebook profile. Her picture was still there. Take this down, she wrote in the comments.

YOU ARE BEAUTIFUL, he replied.

Jacklynn wanted to scream. The point is, I don't want you sharing my stuff on your profile, she wrote. There are boundaries.

She and her friend Bailey were both hosting at Big Whiskey's that day. And maybe it was the adrenaline of the last twenty-four hours or her lack of sleep, but Jacklynn felt downright giddy. The two of them laughed at everything, quoting random memes, saying random stuff.

During her break, she checked Facebook again. Her dad had taken the picture down and was trying to apologize. But he couldn't even get that right. I apology, he'd written.

Jacklynn made up her mind.

She blocked him and then changed her privacy settings.

CONNER

A Room of His Own

It happened out of the blue. Conner came back to Carman one afternoon to find Omar packing his bags. He'd gotten a single in John Jay, and just like that, he was gone.

"I don't know why he left," Conner said. "I was entirely non-confrontational and polite. Or so I thought."

Conner called Jacklynn to tell her the news. She was floored, relieved, ecstatic. Finally, they could talk without interruption. Without loud music or videos blaring. Without parties raging in the background.

The room wasn't quite as homey, now that Omar's stuff was gone, but Jacklynn said this was an opportunity. Why not move Omar's desk? Lower his bed and make it into a couch? Put out the snacks. Flaunt those Pop-Tarts! Use the empty closet to store all the books and board games. Hang up more posters. It was their world building come to life.

Conner's RA warned him against going crazy with the redecorating, since the housing office would likely move someone else in. But Conner doubted this.

"A: Who's going to move into a double?" he said. "Only someone coming from a double would move into a double, and the evil that you know has got to be better than the evil you don't. I'm the unknown evil!"

He seemed proud of this fact.

"And B: Someone from a single isn't going to move into a double. And C: I live on the worst floor in Carman. I hear people in the elevator actively talking about how bad the floor is. Anytime the doors open on two, it's, Oh god. Nobody wants to be here."

Nobody, except for Conner, of course. All of a sudden, Carman was exactly where he wanted to be.

BRIANI & GENEVIEVE

Study Break: Part 1

The weeks leading up to Thanksgiving were stressful, to say the least. Briani had been in Butler Library multiple nights until 2:00 a.m. She'd gotten sick, with a runny nose, cough, and general exhaustion, as though her body had looked her stress in the eye and said, *Fine, you win*. On the phone with her mom, she wondered, *What does a heart attack feel like, because mine is beating so fast*. Also, she was convinced she'd contracted pink eye. Health services said her eyes were just bloodshot from lack of sleep. Leonor called her sister, and Titi Jackie swept in from Washington Heights like a Mother Teresa with herbal tea and soup.

Finally, Briani was on the mend, and on this Thursday night, taking a study break in the dorm. Given her stress level, her room was impressively tidy: the bed made, the desk orderly, some scattered notebooks and shoes on the floor.

There was also an unexpected object hanging off her desk chair: a winter jacket with the Canada Goose crest. "Canada Goose Culture" had become FLI slang, a catch-all term ragging on the affluence of elite campuses. So what was Briani doing with a $650 jacket?

"Genevieve lent it to me," she said, and laughed. "I was like,

'This is yours?' and she said, 'No, girl, my aunt went on a spending spree!'"

There was a knock at the door and Genevieve arrived, bundled in a brown corduroy parka, though she'd only just come from down the hall. The jacket had a kind of hunting vibe, which she'd offset with colorful earrings that dangled well past her shoulders. She'd pulled her hair back in a bun—no time to primp these days. Briani agreed. She'd bundled against the early winter chill in a thrifted John Deere sweatshirt and her Birkenstocks (of course) with gray socks.

"The semester went by so fast!" Briani groaned. "I underestimated. I wish I'd spent more time doing social things."

She giggled. Genevieve giggled. They were giggling out their stress.

"But my parents didn't come to America so I could kiki around," Briani added. Hence her tame social life. And how weird she felt about maybe, possibly deciding to double major in poli-sci and American studies. "I was talking to my friends John and Neely about how cute it would be to major in American studies, and Neely said her dad majored in that, and *he* was saying it's so unemployable."

The girls sat down, Briani at her desk, Genevieve at Brooklyn's desk. "You're upholding the expectations of a whole group of people," Genevieve said. "Especially in this political climate. It's like, because you have what it takes to go to an Ivy League school, you *have* to go to an Ivy League school. I'm glad I'm here, but I wish it felt like more of my choice in the end."

It was hard not to compare her situation to her high school classmates'. Tuition for Saint Ann's was over $50,000 a year (i.e., most kids had an industrial-strength safety net). "They're simply able to say, 'Oh, I'm going to school for art, I'm going to school for acting,'" Genevieve said. "That never felt like a choice for me." And this being New York City, they had crazy social capital. "It's like you're still a senior and you already have this Netflix show or you just graduated and you're already getting nominated for an Oscar."

She wanted to be an actor, had always wanted to act. But when she was younger, her mother said, *You cannot go to Columbia for acting; that's just not what you do. College is an investment, and acting is not a worthwhile investment.*

Genevieve said her mom now denies having said this. But Genevieve maintains it's true. Her mother had a master's degree from Columbia Teachers College and oversaw the English language-arts program at a school in their town. Her grandmother had also been a teacher and even run a pre-K out of her house in Brooklyn.

"It completely shaped my entire middle school and high school attitude about college and my future," she said. "It's a constant tug-of-war." Because her heart said: *You are an actor.* But she was strong in math, so her brain said: *You've got to major in astrophysics or neuroscience.*

This conflict had taught Genevieve an important lesson: Wealth and individualism were linked. That was certainly true of high school social life. Her Saint Ann's friends went to parties and concerts as they pleased; Genevieve's mom was more cautious. But it was also *a* truth of life generally. Wealth meant you could put your happiness first. If you wanted to be an artist, go be an artist. Give it a try. If you failed, you could try something else.

Genevieve longed to put her happiness first, to be that artist. But how could she justify this? Her family had struggled to escape the shadow of slavery and Jim Crow. Through education and hard work, they'd been able to achieve both stability and mobility, to run faster and lift higher. They'd gotten this far and passed the baton to her. With a degree in neuroscience or physics, she'd really be able to take off. Maybe then, when her own kids graduated from high school, they'd have the freedom to claim their happiness, to give their dreams a try.

Briani knew her parents had tried to shield her from financial insecurity. But she knew what was going on—like when the family's cable subscription would disappear or she would be back on the free-and-reduced lunch list. At the moment, José had no idea his daughter was considering an American studies major. She knew it wouldn't go over well. Still, she insisted the pressure to succeed was self-imposed. "These were internal struggles I put on myself," she said. "But I don't want to spend the rest of my life hating what I do. What's the point of having some goofy-looking degree and all this money if you hate your life?"

What did they want to do? Who did they want to be? Every eighteen-year-old asked these questions. The answers were never simple.

"A lot of my family members get that I don't want to work just to make it to the next vacation. But they think I'm naïve," Genevieve said. She shrugged. "And maybe I am, because you have to pay your dues."

She was prepared for constant rejection. She knew she'd have to work a job she didn't love to keep her acting dream alive. She knew she'd get small or silly roles for years until suddenly the universe blessed her with *the* part, the role that catapulted her into the limelight.

Briani said her dues would be working a corporate law job to pay off her law school loans. "I want to practice law to help people, but to get there, you have to do the devil's work, sell your soul," she said. "It kinda sucks."

In a way, the girls were already paying their dues. It was like Maria had said: You have to work twice as hard and be twice as good, because when people look at you, they'll automatically see you as half. Briani was worried about her International Politics final. She was worried about Fro Sci.

They clearly weren't the only ones who worried. Just look at how full the libraries were in the lead-up to finals, and good luck finding an empty seat in one of the reading rooms.

And yet, there were moments—if fleeting—when Briani was able to stop. Moments when she knew she'd achieved something extraordinary. Because look at what she had!

A beautiful college campus decorated with twinkling Christmas lights.

A friend who'd recently lent her an expensive winter coat.

And even her upcoming Fro Sci final, which, annoying as it was, meant that she was a freshman at Columbia University.

From this vista, she saw herself a year ago, applying to college. Back then, her stress had seemed existential. Like the rest of her life was riding on the outcome. When she'd gotten into Columbia, she felt so overwhelmed—and, frankly, so grateful—that she/ called the admissions office to thank them.

Meanwhile, in recent weeks, kids from her high school had been reaching out, asking her for advice on their college applications. We heard about you, they said. Can you help us?

Briani always said yes. "Seeing more and more kids apply to a school like this, it just blows my mind."

As both girls knew, Columbia was not built for Netzahuatls and Thandiwes. And yet, increasingly, names like these populated class rosters, each one attached to a student like Briani and Genevieve. They were kids with complicated but often beautiful histories. Kids who were sculpting a new campus from the inside out.

"There might not necessarily be a space for me here," Briani said. "But I have the right to make that space for myself."

DECEMBER

CONNER

The Elizabeth Warren Letter-Writing Campaign

Over the course of his University Writing seminar, the mandatory essay class for freshmen, Conner had gleaned certain things about William Tracy Jr. There was his physical appearance (tall and Black), his athleticism (he was on the school's basketball team), and his interest in the economy. He talked about Steve Jobs and Warren Buffett. He'd referenced the book *Rich Dad Poor Dad* more than once.

He seemed like a nice guy, though he was also something of a mystery to Conner. Earlier in the semester, they'd been reading the essays "Sweatshop Sublime" and "Maid to Order" and discussing whether it was ethical to hire domestic labor. Conner recalled William saying kind of nonchalantly that maids cleaned his parents' house, and it wasn't a big deal. Conner had no idea at what level of wealth maids became commonplace, but it seemed like maybe a lot? He marveled at how unconcerned William seemed.

"Like he was reflecting on it, but wasn't really troubled," Conner said. "He was just like, 'Oh, yeah, I guess I can see how having a maid can be problematic.'"

Fast-forward to their final assignment of the semester: to write an op-ed.

"I don't think you guys are going to like my argument," William said when the instructor called on him. This got everybody's attention. "Rich kids should be able to buy their spots at top-tier universities to create more scholarship money for low-income kids," he said.

After a moment of shocked silence, the instructor said, "Well, that's a pretty big claim." And then there proceeded to be a polite discussion about the idea. A few people were like, But you see why that would be a problem, right?

Conner didn't say anything. He was still at a loss for words.

He was thinking that he appreciated his instructor's ability to create an environment where students felt comfortable testing outlandish ideas.

He was also thinking how outlandishly offensive the idea was. Whatever you wanted to say about merit in admissions or the lack of it, Conner had worked his butt off to get here with very little privilege and even fewer resources. He knew he was walking into a wealthy environment, but William's proposal was next-level shocking.

Still, he felt bad for having any negative thoughts about William Tracy Jr., because what had the guy ever done to him?

A little while later, students paired up to discuss their op-ed topics. Conner found himself talking about William's essay with the girl sitting next to him. Mackenzie: tall, blond, possibly from North Carolina. From William's crazy proposal, conversation meandered to other unrealistic (if less offensive) proposals, like how Bernie Sanders and Elizabeth Warren wanted to cancel all student debt and make public colleges free. This inevitably led to a debate over who was more progressive. Mackenzie was in the Warren camp all the way. She said, "Hey, I'm going to this letter-writing event for Warren, if you wanted to come."

"That sounds cool," Conner said. "I'd go." They exchanged phone numbers.

And then class was over, and everybody filed out to go and write their op-eds.

But the more Conner thought about that class, the less he was thinking about William Tracy Jr. and the more he was thinking about Jacklynn, and how she'd react when she learned that a woman named Mackenzie, who was tall and blond and possibly from North Carolina, had invited him to a social event.

He didn't think Mackenzie was asking him out. Surely, she wasn't hitting on him. She was trying to drum up support for Elizabeth Warren. Obviously.

Still, when he tried to think of what he'd tell Jacklynn, to prevent her from feeling jealous or upset, he couldn't come up with anything. A degree of bad feeling seemed inevitable. But *not* saying anything to Jacklynn wasn't an option; he'd feel way too weird about that, like he was trying to hide something. So in the end, he took the easiest course of action.

He didn't go.

It wasn't worth the trouble. And the more that Conner thought about it, the more he hoped Bernie would win.

BRIANI & CONNER

Finals

She had to learn all of this:

He had to learn all of this:

What can you really say about finals? They suck. Even when they appear to be manageable or have some kind of creative bent, it's just an illusion. Finals are meant to test what you know (or should know), and no matter how hard you study, you'll come up short (or feel like you do). The best you could do with finals was remember that time marched forward. Past the reading and the highlighting and the note-taking. Past the study sessions and continuous cups of coffee. Past stumbling back from Butler at 2:00 a.m. Past feeling like your brain simply wasn't big enough to fit all the information you were supposed to cram into it.

Just remember: This, too, shall pass. Soon enough you'll be on the other side. Finals: Finished.

But first, there was Dr. Pemberton, the anthro professor who said the final would be a take-home. Conner was delighted. Piece of cake. Even better, he had a full two weeks to get it done.

Then Pemberton laid out the specifics: three prompts of four pages each, so actually a twelve-pager. And the questions were bizarre, like:

It is 1905. Max Weber is suffering from terrible nightmares. He seeks help from that controversial pioneer of the unconscious and specialist in dreams, Dr. Sigmund Freud. What, precisely, tran-spires?

And

Michel Foucault is applying for a job in the most famous anthro-pology department in the world. Does he get the job?

And

Claude Lévi-Strauss is running from Europe (from the "Western" mindset, the French philosophical scene, the bourgeois imaginar, fascist politics, and all the rest), but he takes the wrong boat and stumbles into West Virginia. Well, alright! What would he write in this particular, strange new place? What would he make of thangs?

All of this was both super interesting to consider and not fun at all.

And, meanwhile, he had a Lit Hum exam and a French exam and a film exam and a University Writing paper, all of which meant he looked up one afternoon and realized the anthro exam was due like the next day. So Conner loaded up his study music of choice—the soundtrack to *Conan the Barbarian*—and sat down to work.

And he worked.

And he worked.

And he banged his head against the wall.

And he worked some more.

For eight hours straight.

(He ate something and slept.)

He woke up and got back to work.

For another eight hours.

(Did he eat or sleep again? He couldn't remember.)

He powered through for another eight hours until, at 8:00 a.m. on December 16th, he hit save for the last time and uploaded the document.

He had four hours to spare. Not bad at all.

WINTER
BREAK

OZARK &
SPRINGFIELD, MO

Steak 'N Shake: Part 1

Compared to high school breaks, winter breaks in college felt luxurious. You'd go home around the third week in December and literally have zero schoolwork until second semester started just after Martin Luther King Day. A six-week vacation—could you imagine? Conner barely knew what to do with all this free time.

And so, on a weekday night in the middle of January 2020, he gathered with his friends at their go-to Springfield dinner spot: Steak 'n Shake. His friend Sean was turning nineteen, and the group had come out in force to celebrate: Sean; his girlfriend, Claire; Schween; Jack; Taylor; Jacklynn; and Conner.

They pushed a bunch of two-tops together and dug into their burgers. But by the time the fries were dwindling, the oratorial combat between Conner and his friend Taylor was just ramping up. They'd gotten into a debate about rivers. Conner happened to mention that Columbia offered a class on the subject: Rivers, Politics and Power in the United States. And this seemed to offend Taylor's sensibilities, because rivers? Boring!

To which Conner countered, "Did Caesar cross the Rubicon *Lake*? I don't think so!"

Then, somehow, this gave way to the question of whether Branson, Missouri, about forty-five miles south of Springfield, was worth anybody's time. It was one of those places all the friends had been but didn't frequent.

When they started in, Jacklynn—who'd clearly been keeping one ear on the conversation—interrupted her discussion with Claire at the other end of the table to roll her eyes and say, "Branson? Conner, why are you choosing that metaphorical river to die in?"

"Because Dolly Parton's there," Conner said.

Which was a stretch. Dolly Parton's Stampede Dinner Attraction, an elaborate horse-themed theatrical dinner-show, was in Branson. Though whether Dolly Parton had actually been there herself was questionable.

"That's it?" Taylor said.

"Weird Al owns a theater in Branson," Conner said. This was possibly not true. "And there are all the museums."

"The Titanic Museum, I guess," Taylor conceded. "And the Bald Knobbers were from there." He seemed to have given up on his side of the argument.

Jacklynn leaned back over. "Oh, Conner, get on your soapbox!"

"It's a fascinating piece of Ozarks history," Conner said, as though he were a museum docent. "Whereas many of the connections to Missouri and the Civil War are very negative, the Bald Knobbers were a vigilante group in the area that attacked the KKK and fended off Confederate militias. I'm very proud of that fact."

Taylor said a distant relative had been a Bald Knobber and was eventually hanged in the village square. Conner said a lot of locals believed the Bald Knobbers had Confederate roots—which, unfortunately, some locals considered a good thing. And wouldn't it blow their minds to know the vigilantes were actually anti-slavery—aka, the good guys?

This was a rhetorical question. They were a bunch of liberals (and a couple of socialists) who'd gone to high school in one of the country's most conservative regions. Their county literally had "Christian" in its name. In 2016, Donald Trump won it with around 74 percent of the vote.

"It's the Bible Belt," Jacklynn said. "I have a really big family, so when my opinions differ, it's definitely something I keep my mouth shut on."

Conner said his mom changed her political opinions depending on the man she was dating or what she'd read on Facebook. She'd voted for Obama, then Gary Johnson, the Libertarian. Conner said his grandparents believed in a woman's right to choose and gun control. But their fiscal conservatism dictated their voting behavior every time.

So how had Conner and his friends managed to become Democrats?

"Compassion," Jacklynn said. "As opposed to being racist and hateful."

Interlude: Devil-Worshipping, Elitist, Communist Yogis

There weren't many majority-progressive communities at Ozark High School, but Conner managed to find one of them. His junior year he enrolled in the school's International Baccalaureate World School program, otherwise known as "IB." The program officially launched at Ozark in 2013 to meet the needs of high-achieving kids who weren't getting enough from the school's few AP courses.

"It pushes them to be a world citizen, not just an American citizen," said Sara Floyd, who directed IB at Ozark and taught its Global Politics course. "For our students, who are here and land-locked in southwest Missouri, it gets them out of the mentality that this is the only place that exists."

An IB high school diploma is offered at more than 960 American schools and more than 3,000 schools around the world. It was originally designed for the kids of diplomats. Students could leave an IB program in China and enter one in France and pick up exactly where they left off. The curriculum was rigorous.

"It requires a large amount of self-reflection and critical

thinking," Floyd said. "Examining other people's ideas and not just getting tunnel vision into our own." She said that American history and politics were often presented from a global perspective: the role America has played in other countries and their conflicts. "Not that we are right or wrong but why is it happening," Floyd explained.

But a lot of people felt that America (and the traditional narrative of American history as written by those Dead White Males) was always "right." And so, even though Ozark's IB program was supported by the principal and vice principal at the time, it got a "huge amount of pushback," according to Floyd.

People called it Communist.

They called it anti-American.

Floyd said IB did not ask students to give up Christianity. It did not try to dictate anyone's political affiliation.

But okay, Conner conceded that the curriculum pushed against the grain. IB was about exploring ambiguity, and Ozark was the opposite. "Hard right, pro-life. No ambiguity whatsoever," he said. "Even women here talk about the 'women's role in the home.'" He pointed to James River, the Assemblies of God megachurch with four locations in the Ozark area that boasted around fifteen thousand weekly worshippers (plus seventy-four thousand more who watched online). "They've got two Starbucks inside the main facility," he said, as though to demonstrate the church's dominance. "And they rant about how doing yoga lets demons into your soul." Standard Pentecostal stuff.

Conner said Sara Floyd taught yoga, and after the church started preaching against it, people stopped coming to her classes. "The amount of sway they hold is ridiculous," he said.

He was disappointed that the senior class voted to hold its graduation there instead of the John Q Hammons Arena.

In other words, IB was not a natural fit for Ozark.

Many (though not all) IB students self-identified as liberal. Maybe because of this, people called the program elitist. (Because, you know, where there are liberals, there are obviously elites.) Conner didn't think the accusation of elitism was about anti-intellectualism but more about the perceived "special privileges" IB students had. For instance, he organized a benefit concert on behalf of Helen Keller International and Oxfam for his Global Politics class. Kids then called him elitist. They were like, Why are you so special that you get to use the whole auditorium?

IB was also considered elitist because it was small. The year Conner graduated, only thirteen of these students, Conner among them, actually received the official IB diploma. The other thirty-three simply took a smattering of IB classes alongside their regular courses. But this was the point, according to Floyd. Literally anyone could take an IB class, try something new. You didn't need to be a first-class nerd to hack it in IB. Jacklynn had taken IB Film her junior and senior years and loved that it was creatively challenging.

Finally, people called it elitist by saying it was just for rich, white kids. It wasn't the strongest argument, considering that 89 percent of the school was white. As for the rich part, well, you could talk to Conner about that.

Conner admitted there had been some IB students with a "holier-than-thou" attitude, but, he said, "Sara Floyd dealt with that."

Floyd said IB asked all students—liberal and conservative—to question their assumptions. "We talk a whole lot in IB about why we can't seem to get along," she said. "We're always open to knowing other people's opinions. We can disagree respectfully and remain passionate about our own beliefs."

She felt today's Ozark students, while very much rooted in their home and culture, were increasingly open-minded. "I really do believe that the generation that's in seventh grade through the recent college graduates will be the generation that saves us from this debacle of our political environment," she said.

Steak 'N Shake: Part 2

Back at Steak 'n Shake, the friends said they weren't sure if Gen Z was so different. Conner believed 60 percent of the school had voted for Trump in its mock election, with the next largest bloc supporting Gary Johnson, the Libertarian. Taylor worried Gen Z was swinging right. He pointed out the popularity of Joe Rogan, who had no problem normalizing people like Alex Jones, the conspiracy theorist who called the Sandy Hook Elementary School shooting fake. He said they listened to Jordan Peterson, who promoted transphobia and hate speech.

"The Gay-Straight Alliance had a day to remember trans lives," Conner said. "And a bunch of kids wore shirts mocking that." On another occasion, Conner's lab partner, who was also the school's running back, asked him if he believed in God. Conner said not particularly. Then the running back asked whether Conner could love a son who was gay.

Conner said yes.

The running back considered this, then said, "I don't think I would."

"He may have been messing with me," Conner said. "But the remainder of the three years he was in high school, he would have had to be in character the whole time, so I doubt it."

Taylor was mocked for wearing a Bernie shirt.

Their friend Jack was called a Communist.

Taylor said he'd actually been an anarchist as a kid.

"Which makes sense," Conner said, "because you don't acknowledge the significance of Branson or rivers."

"I do acknowledge rivers' significance," Taylor said. "I just don't have the interest in taking a class on it."

Conner gave him a look, like, *Suit yourself.*

But nonsense aside, where did they come down on Gen Z?

Jacklynn said her American Sign Language Instructor at the community college was openly gay, and it didn't cause the slightest stir on the first day of class.

"She was all excited for her fun lesbian teacher," Conner said. "We're getting better. It's a big shift."

"Absolutely," Taylor said.

So was their generation less racist and homophobic?

"I hope so," Conner said.

Family History

Earlier that day, Conner and Jacklynn had gone to the Battlefield Mall so that Jacklynn could buy some jeans. Conner had been quite the dutiful boyfriend, ferrying different sizes and colors to her in the Macy's dressing room. After that, they popped into a couple of other stores, including a pop culture bonanza called Boxed Lunch, where Jacklynn bought a sweatshirt that said DUNDER MIFFLIN and had a picture of "Pam's Painting" from *The Office* on the back. She skipped Altar'd State, a clothing store for "preppy Christian girls," where her best friend Caroline used to work.

Afterward, they climbed into Stacey's Toyota 4Runner for a Springfield city tour. The car was eighteen years old and, as Jacklynn explained, had once been a receptacle for their fossilized relationship items: stickers, dashboard knickknacks, and key chains. But they'd cleared out most of them before Conner left for school.

Now they drove through the city, discussing Stacey and Ayden's housing situation. After her last breakup, Stacey had moved in to her parents' Springfield home. But they were eager to sell the place. For months now, the move had been coming "soon." But "soon" was a state of suspended animation.

Stacey had scouted places—which meant she'd sent Conner to

scout places—only to decide she couldn't afford them. Or didn't like them. Conner drove past an apartment complex called the Polo Club, where the family had lived about seven years before. Apartment Ratings gave it a C+, but it wasn't bad, Conner said. It was definitely on the list. A two-bedroom, two-bath apartment ran you about $600 a month. And the floor plans were compact, which would be good for Stacey. Too many doors and windows weren't good for her PTSD.

"She was talking about that before we went to the mall," Jacklynn said. "How she doesn't like the number of entrances or windows at your grandparents' house."

"She feels vulnerable," Conner said. "It's totally understandable. Definitely a part of her history and trauma."

When Conner was three, his father died of a drug overdose. Conner didn't remember him. "I was told he was pretty smart," he said. "That he wanted to join the Air Force."

"Your mom said he was a really good dad," Jacklynn said.

"He was a good waiter," Conner said. "He worked at the Tower Club, which I think closed down? He worked at the Mexican Villa with my mother. A bunch of other odd jobs. I don't know a lot. My parents met in high school. They were in circles that got them into their addictions. They were using a lot of different things."

"Opioids," Jacklynn said.

"They tried to get out of it," Conner said.

After his father passed away, his mom went to a clinic and got sober. A year or two later, she met a man—the person who would become Ayden's father. Conner didn't know much about him. He didn't remember much, didn't *witness* much. "Though I guess any amount was too much," he said. "I saw something . . ."

This was all he would say.

He had no memory of the police coming to their home.

He had no memory of them taking Stacey's boyfriend away.

What he does remember is that he was asked to testify before a judge—and how much he didn't want to.

So he didn't.

"I was five," he said. "And, yeah."

They drove in silence, the wheels turning over asphalt.

The crime his mother's boyfriend committed had a name: sexual and physical assault. The prison sentence was long. The impact was deep. Conner didn't think about it every day, but his mom did. "I think she's come to terms," he said. "But it's not something you can get over."

"She had the relapse," Jacklynn said. "Right before you went to school."

"She's five months sober now," Conner said. She was responsible for her kids—especially Adyen—and she knew it. She loved them. She wanted the best for them.

"Are we going by the stadium?" Jacklynn asked.

"Sure," Conner said, and turned at the next light.

"It's for our Minor League Baseball team," Jacklynn explained. "The Springfield Cardinals. When I was little and my mom used to take me there, I thought she was taking me to St. Louis to see the actual Cardinals. So when I was fifteen and my mom broke the news that I'd never been to St. Louis, I was very shocked."

"You thought *this* was St. Louis?" Conner said. Like, *How could anyone mistake the measly streets of Springfield for the big, bustling city?*

"No!" Jacklynn was offended. "I thought I'd *been* to St. Louis as a kid."

"Oh," Conner said.

They drove over to the Springfield campus of OTC, where Jacklynn would be taking most of her sophomore-year classes. And almost across the street, Missouri State University, where she planned to transfer after she got her associate's degree. She pointed out the theater where touring companies performed. Next week, her mom was taking her to see *Les Misérables*, one of her favorite shows.

Conner said the breakup with Stacey's most recent ex caused her relapse. Plus the issues with her medication, which sometimes caused hallucinations. Plus fears that her other ex—Adyen's father—would try to take Ayden in a custody battle.

"Which is ridiculous," Conner said. "He sexually assaulted her and has been in prison for years." Conner looked up at the street signs alongside MSU's campus. "I wonder if I should have gone down further," he said, like we'd been talking directions the whole time. Then, "John Goodman went to MSU." At nineteen, Conner was a master of compartmentalization.

Jacklynn wasn't so bad at this herself. She hadn't heard from her father since the Facebook incident. Her uncle, an exterminator who worked at her dad's former housing complex, said he'd been kicked out for breaking various rules. Apparently, her father now had a job cutting meat at the grocery store.

"Stick It in Your Ear is down here," Conner interrupted, and pointed. "That's a good music shop."

"There's the YMCA," Conner said.

"We have one of those?" Jacklynn asked.

"We have several," Conner assured her.

Jacklynn pointed out a large butterfly mural.

Conner pointed out another mural memorializing the Trail of Tears, some craft breweries, an independent movie theater, and the Springfield History Museum. "We do have a lot of history," he said. "And not all of it good." He pulled a U-turn and they started back toward the mall.

Big Whiskey's

Conner and Jacklynn planned their first date sophomore year, during rehearsal for *Charlie and the Chocolate Factory*. Conner was Augustus Gloop, and Jacklynn was his mom, which was super awkward since they had a crush on each other. Around that time, Conner learned that Jacklynn had never seen the original Star Wars trilogy. He was shocked. Such a lapse required immediate remedy. So in between scenes, he asked if she'd like to see the movie and get dinner that night. Jacklynn screwed up her courage and said, "Is this a date?" And Conner said, "Yeah, if you want it to be."

But the timing was tricky. Jacklynn had never been on a real date, and she wasn't sure how her mother would react. Sherry was incredibly protective—you might say *over*protective. She was also out of town at a prayer conference and had put Jacklynn's sister Crystal in charge. It did not feel like the best time for Jacklynn to tell her family that she was going out with a boy.

But a boy had asked her to dinner and she wasn't about to turn him down.

So she lied to her sister and said that she was going home with a friend after school. Then she turned off her phone so as not to interrupt the romantic moment with an accidental butt dial.

They went to a diner chain called the Village Inn. It was two minutes from school, perched on a concrete hill overlooking the Pizza Hut and the Mitchun Tires. They'd just ordered their food when Jacklynn suddenly heard her sister's voice.

"Yeah, I see her," her sister was saying into the phone. Then Crystal all but dragged Jacklynn out of the restaurant.

It was mortifying. Even more so, because Jacklynn's backpack was in Conner's car, so she had to go back into the restaurant and ask Conner to come out and unlock it.

Apparently, Crystal had been trying to call, but since Jacklynn's phone kept going to voice mail, she started to worry. She texted Sherry, to say that Jacklynn was MIA. At that moment, though, Sherry was at an internationally televised sermon. In a state of panic akin to cardiac arrest, Sherry jumped up and, in front of the packed church and Lord knows how many viewers around the globe, squeezed herself out to the aisle. Meanwhile, Crystal was driving Jacklynn home, saying, "You're lucky Mom is at Jesus camp right now."

With their date cut so rudely short, Conner sat in his car and listened to "The Sound of Silence," feeling a little bit sad and a little disappointed. "I thought I'd never see her again," he said. "I mean, outside of drama."

When Jacklynn got home, she typed her mother an essay-style letter of apology, complete with a thesis and three discrete body paragraphs. Sherry still keeps the letter folded inside a prophetic prayer book called *Jesus Calling*.

Three years later, Sherry and Jacklynn sat in a corner booth at Big Whiskey's in Ozark, waiting for Conner to arrive. Jacklynn wore her new Dunder Mifflin sweatshirt. Sherry was a walking advertisement for the Kansas City Chiefs and, unintentionally, for Ozark's politics: red to the power of infinity. Suffice it to say that mother and daughter (let alone daughter's boyfriend) did not discuss politics. But that was okay. Sherry had grown to love Conner—and loved Jacklynn with Conner. You could tell because Sherry teased the people she cared for most. (Example: As they waited for Conner to arrive, Jacklynn said she'd made a friend in chemistry class and Sherry retorted, "Aww, finally you have one!")

Now they watched Conner pull into the lot and park twenty feet away from the entrance despite a dozen empty spots right outside the door.

"Oh, Conner, what are you doing, dude?" Sherry wondered aloud, and shook her head. Her voice was gravelly, the result of a decades-long cigarette habit.

"That's why I call him dumb," Jacklynn said with a shrug.

"He's a brilliant idiot," Sherry replied.

They laughed. Both agreed Conner was probably the smartest person they knew.

Conner finally arrived and slid into the booth, his cheeks flushed as though he'd been running. Inadvertently, he took a gulp of Sherry's water.

The server arrived. "Do you need a water?" she asked Conner.

"*I* do!" Sherry said. "Because he took mine."

Then she ordered a margarita, because she almost never went

out to eat, let alone drink a cocktail. But a dinner out with Jacklynn *and* Conner—both on break from college—was a special occasion. She asked Conner if he was coming home for the summer and looked quite happy when he said yes.

Sherry's support for their relationship was a big deal. She and Jacklynn had worked hard to build a loving, stable home after Jacklynn's father left. They'd created a kind of cocoon. It was this—not just the expense—that had kept Jacklynn at home.

"We just came to a time in our life where we can appreciate things without her father," Sherry said. "That's huge. The abuse, the fighting was just horrible for her. Now we can finally be together." Sherry paused as though she might tear up. "For her to leave me and go off somewhere, you wouldn't get to see the life that could have been. But"—Sherry cleared her throat—"I miss him." She nodded at Conner. "I know they're on the phone until the wee hours."

"She yells at me about it," Jacklynn said flatly.

"I miss having him over for dinner. I didn't know for months that he didn't live with us."

"Every day for two years we didn't spend more than one or two days apart," Jacklynn said.

This didn't sound like a rebuke, but it was hard to tell. Conner didn't react.

Sherry worked in the disabled dependent department at a large health-care company. It wasn't a career that she'd necessarily imagined for herself. In fact, she'd always intended to get a college degree. She'd been accepted to MSU after high school, even secured a dorm room with her best friend. But the summer after high school, she went to Illinois to see her father—a man who hadn't been around very much. And he said, *You don't need college. Stay here, I'll get you a job. You can have a career off the bat.* So that's what Sherry did.

But it wasn't long before her father, a life insurance salesman, headed out on the road, leaving Sherry alone in a large house. It wasn't what she'd signed up for. So she left, snuck out her stuff. She was eighteen and, as she put it, "stupid." She moved in with her fiancé. Four years later, he was killed in a car accident.

After this, she would marry, then divorce, then marry again. Jacklynn was the one child she'd had from these marriages, but she loved Jacklynn's half sisters, including Crystal, like her own.

No, she hadn't dreamed of working in insurance. But she'd had good work for thirty-three years. Hard work, too. It was gut-wrenching, she said, listening to parents talk about their disabled grown children. And not being able to help, because for whatever reason the state said they didn't qualify for coverage. "It's a hard job to have when you have compassion," she said. "Your heart gets involved."

Sherry always wanted to be an archaeologist. Somebody who put things back together. "My forte is I fix things," she said proudly, and Jacklynn nodded, as though to say, *You've never seen a fixer like my mom.*

"My mother taught me more about cars than my father," Jacklynn said. "You fixed the fridge and the TV. You're about to fix the microwave."

"Does she have to go to school to get a job?" Sherry wondered aloud. "Nowadays, kids going to school are getting cheated. Sometimes the job market is there and sometimes it's not." But as much as Sherry wanted her daughter to be practical, she also gushed over Jacklynn's many less-than-practical talents: her writing and her art. She thought about her own mother, a world-class whistler, who would whistle old songs while she cleaned the house on Saturdays. Literally whistle while she worked. The whistle would waft through the house and Sherry felt buoyed, protected. Perhaps Sherry's appreciation for Jacklynn's creativity originated here. The idea that art could comfort, could even fulfill.

"She has enough potential," Sherry said, as though she was sharing a secret. "The things she writes. Unbelievable. The child is writing songs. Good songs. Absolutely beautiful. She's got art." She turned to Jacklynn. "I tell her, 'I'm sorry, you don't have to have it all figured out.'" It sounded like this was a familiar argument between them. And unexpected, since it was so often the parents pushing the kids to make a choice, have a plan.

As far as Sherry was concerned, she'd be happy with anything Jacklynn decided to do as long as Jacklynn stayed nearby. "If we're in a twenty-five-mile radius, we're cool," she said.

"You know the film industry is here," Jacklynn joked. The future of their relationship posed an issue: Conner dreamed of becoming a filmmaker, which meant he wouldn't be settling down in Missouri. And that meant Jacklynn would have to join him, likely in New York or LA.

"Ozark," Conner said half-heartedly, "The Hollywood of the Midwest."

Jacklynn looked a little sheepish. "It's just a dream, but all my life, I've pictured being rich. Living in New York in a nice house, doing my dream job, being mildly famous." She said she was struggling to pick a major. She kept panicking, because what if the things she loved weren't lucrative?

Sherry nodded as though to say, *See what I mean?*

"I don't think about the future ever," Conner said.

Jacklynn said, "I've tried to ask him about it, but then he just jokes about having three mansions in Bali."

Conner said he could only see as far as an MFA program in film after college.

"You know it'll come through, don't ya?" Sherry said. She seemed to have more faith in Conner than Conner did.

"I think about it, but I don't *think* about it," he said.

"You have a direction," Sherry said.

Conner admitted the future made him nervous. Because pursuing film meant his financial prospects were a big question mark. He preferred to focus on the now, study as hard as he could.

Sherry said she liked to think about Conner and Jacklynn sending their kids to college. She liked the idea of them being "second-generation" instead of the first.

"Our kids would be really cool," Jacklynn said. "Interested in nerdy things—art and D&D."

"I hope they'll be smart, too," Sherry said. "Because they'll have to take care of their grandma."

LAWRENCEVILLE, GA

Safe at Home

When Briani first got home, it was strange to be back in her childhood bed. It was so quiet, without the sounds of the dorm: the hallways populated at all hours, Brooklyn turning over in her sleep, typing on her laptop. But man, did Briani look forward to a full twelve hours. She didn't realize how exhausted she was until she dropped her bags inside the front door. All this weight fell away: the stress of constantly keeping up, keeping ahead.

She'd jumped into the arms of her best friend, Maia, and hugged her parents for what seemed like hours.

It felt like safety. Literally home base. Because just as finals were starting, there'd been this terrible event.

December 11th, a Wednesday night. Briani was coming home from church and her phone started pinging with messages from friends: Are you alright? Be careful. Stay safe. Brooklyn called. She sounded panicked. "Where are you?"

A girl had been stabbed in Morningside Park, adjacent to campus.

The text messages from campus safety were incredibly vague. Nobody knew what was going on. Only later did they learn that the victim was a Barnard student named Tessa Majors, a freshman from Charlottesville, Virginia. She was walking through the park when three teenage boys attacked her. She tried to fight them off and was stabbed in the chest several times after biting one boy on the finger. The park sloped downward along a kind of cliffside, and Tessa had dragged herself up dozens of bluestone stairs in search of safety. An interminable climb. She made it as far as the security guard station at 116th street before she collapsed. How long did she lie there bleeding until a guard appeared? She was still conscious when he found her, but she'd been stabbed in the heart. It was already too late.

Briani had been through Morningside Park many times. It was beautiful and quiet, geographically dramatic. A pleasant shortcut to her favorite bakery in Harlem or an ideal place to sit and study on a warm fall day. During orientation, the school said never to walk there at night, and she hadn't. But it was just before 7:00 p.m. when Tessa was attacked. Dark, yes, but not late. And now, lying in her Georgia bedroom, Briani wondered, *How safe is New York? How safe do I really feel?* Her roommate Brooklyn carried a knife and pepper spray. Her friend Rachel pointed out that the guard in the lobby of John Jay was often just listening to music, not paying attention to who went in and out.

She thought of the small, potentially serious missteps that could happen to you in the city. Just a few months ago, Briani got lost on her way to a Friendsgiving in Harlem. She arrived at the building, slipped inside behind another resident, and went to the apartment number she'd written down. The door was unlocked and as she entered, she wondered, *Why is it so quiet in here? Where is everyone?* She walked down the hall until she saw a man, his back turned. The realization came at her like a slap. Briani hightailed it out of there.

Right apartment. Wrong building.

It was super embarrassing. But in the end, just a funny story, the kind of ridiculous thing that could only happen to you in New York. And see? Everything turned out fine. In New York, it was easy to think, *I'll just walk through the park after dark this one time.* And nothing bad happened, so you'd do it again. A false sense of security is what they called it.

And sure, terrible, tragic things happened everywhere. But life at home was just so normal, so totally removed from the city. Her brother, Joseph, had gotten into Kennesaw State, less than an hour from Lawrenceville. Briani was sad not to have seen the joy of his acceptance up close. So she was trying to make up for her absence, hugging her mom a lot. She was trying to pick up slack: washing dishes and vacuuming while her parents were at the restaurant. She had no schoolwork, literally nothing but time. Her friends who'd gone to school locally didn't relish these vacations. They saw their parents frequently, felt smothered at home. Briani wanted to absorb her parents' comfort, store it up for the future. Second semester would be here before she knew it. And she would be back in Manhattan, trying to find her balance as the city's uncertainty swirled around her like a cyclone.

Speak English!

Sometimes the South surprised you. It's 2007, and Briani is six. Her parents have taken the family to an amusement park, and they are all standing in line at the swinging pirate ship—the one that rocks you almost vertical before it turns you into a human pendulum.

José is talking to Leonor when a lady behind them says it: words that are so cliché, you can hardly believe anybody bothers to waste the oxygen.

"You're in America," the lady says. "Speak English!"

José isn't one to start things, but Leonor—don't mess with her. So she says, "Don't talk to us like that." And the lady, she gets angry, starts mouthing off. Briani watches this, worried that they'll be kicked out of line, maybe even out of the park.

Only then, the unexpected happens. The ride operator comes over and says to the lady, "Ma'am, I need you to calm down."

But she doesn't. She keeps on yelling and complaining. And then the next unexpected thing happens: They kick *her* out. Tell her she can't go on the ride. And, amazingly, the other people in line clap.

Briani remembers this moment so clearly, how everyone

cheered when the racist woman was ordered to leave. This was justice, indelible in Briani's mind for its rarity.

More often, though, the story had a different ending. Right after Christmas, while Briani was home for break, the family went to see *Jumanji: The Next Level*, starring the Rock. Briani had wanted to see *Little Women*, but her brother was like, *Nope*. (Not that she'd really expected the others to be enthusiastic about a feminist period drama. But a girl can dream.) The multiplex was crowded, so Leonor and the kids headed inside while José parked.

Immediately, Briani felt the tension in the line for the movie like a rubber band stretched to the snapping point: everyone worried about getting a good seat, overstuffed from Christmas dinner, and annoyed at too much family time. There was not an abundance of holiday spirit.

And here came José to join his family. *Excuse me, pardon me, thank you.*

A man said, "You're cutting."

Briani turned around. There was a couple behind them: white, midtwenties. It was the boyfriend who'd spoken.

José shook his head. "No," he said. "My family's right here."

"Who the fuck do you think you're talking to?" the boyfriend demanded.

Briani stiffened. This was escalating fast. She and Joseph looked at each other, a single word unspoken between them: *racist.*

José, still calm, said, "I just said 'excuse me.'"

The man was pure anger: the expression on his face, the tone of his voice. "Don't talk to me like that," he snapped. "Don't you talk to me like that."

The girlfriend said, "Let's stop fighting."

But the guy wasn't interested. "Do we need to take this outside?"

"I'm sorry if I came off to you like that," José said. "I was just trying to get to my family."

Briani and Joseph exchanged another look. She could tell that her brother was thinking, *Fuck that guy*. Inside, Briani quivered with emotion.

She wanted to scream at the man.

She wasn't going to stand for this.

This. Wasn't. Okay.

But she couldn't move. Her dad was so calm. Even though she knew the anger was surely there, thick and hard. But José was refusing to expose even a molecule of it.

"Are we okay?" José asked.

The man scowled. "Yeah."

Then the line started moving and they all filed into the theater.

After that, José was quiet. Back home, Briani tried to cheer him up, sent him photos of pasta with the words *bon appétit* and *buongiorno*. Just to be silly. But later, when she and Joseph pressed their dad, José insisted the guy was just a jerk. There were lots of jerks in the world and they weren't all racists.

Briani texted Maia, and Maia agreed with her: definitely racist.

Exactly, Briani replied. She sent a string of rants to her friends. She needed to sound off to somebody. She was mad at herself for not speaking up. And she was frustrated with her parents. Not because they'd turned the other cheek, but for refusing to see the interaction for what it was. It wasn't that they never acknowledged racism. When her mom was laid off from her job of twelve years, she told the family it was mostly Black and brown employees who got the cut. But now, whenever Briani referred to "Trump supporters," when discussing politics, José and Leonor just shook their heads. They didn't want to hear it.

"It goes back to that survival thing," Briani explained later. "Like, from their point of view, we're just trying to make it here. But that comes at the expense of your dignity. It's hard to see."

Her parents worried she was being brainwashed at school, that Columbia was too woke, the students and professors quick to dismiss contrary opinions. But even if that was true in some cases, the college culture hadn't shaped Briani's worldview. Life had. What she saw—and how she felt—every day. Had Trump done anything to improve the family business? And even if he had, could that ever compensate for inciting so much hatred against people like her?

She tried to tell her dad, "You've been through too much to accept someone dehumanizing you and calling you a criminal." But then she felt herself starting to cry and decided to drop it. She didn't want to waste her few precious weeks home with her family arguing about politics.

Current Events

In early January 2020, Briani was reading the news on her phone: *The Atlanta Journal Constitution*, *BuzzFeed*, and *The New York Times*, maybe a bunch of other sites. Among the headlines was one that read "China Grapples with Mystery Pneumonia-Like Illness." She didn't pay much attention to it and was soon onto stories about the Australia fires and Harvey Weinstein.

Existential Crisis

Meanwhile, Briani was having a mini existential crisis. One night, shortly before she was due to return to New York, she sat on her bed watching YouTube videos, one after the next. They had titles like:

"What I Wish I'd Known When Starting Law School," and

"Should I Become a Lawyer? (the honest truth)," and

"The Truth About a Big Law Firm Salary."

It was just like she and Genevieve had discussed: How could you possibly reconcile the need to be self-sufficient, with the need to make a difference, with the need to be happy? Because according to YouTube, if she became a lawyer, she was going to be rich, selfish, and miserable. So what mattered most?

Self-Sufficiency.

Shortly before she'd come home for break, she'd gotten an email from the financial aid office, saying she was eligible for something called the Deans' Student Assistance Fund. The school would give her up to $200 for a winter coat or other basic necessities.

Briani didn't have a winter coat. (Not after she returned the Canada Goose to Genevieve.) So she took the money and bought a North Face puffer. Leonor was not happy to hear it. "We don't need handouts or charity," she said. Briani didn't see it that way. She just wanted to be warm, and the school was offering. Then again, wouldn't it be preferable to become a lawyer and then tell her mother: *I bought this coat with my hard-earned cash, and here's a matching one for you. Sorry if it's too bougie.* Obviously, the answer was yes.

Making a Difference.

In one of the videos, a girl said she wanted to become a lawyer to help people. And Briani thought, "That's me!" But then the girl said, "If that's really your mission, are you sure becoming a lawyer is the best way?"

If Briani wanted to make a difference and be self-sufficient, she'd need to join a big corporate firm and hope that now and then they'd pass her some pro bono work. But mostly, she'd be doing what? Helping rich people get richer? Helping rich people screw over poor people? No thanks.

Happiness.

She needed a backup plan—or maybe just a new plan. She started scouring the Columbia course catalog: English, history, film, media studies. She loved fashion. What if she could work at a magazine—combine her love of clothes with her love of writing? Why didn't Columbia have a design major?

By the time her mom got home from the business that night, Briani was a mess, stressed, confused. Leonor tried to talk her down. "You have so much time," she said. "You don't need to decide now."

But Briani couldn't escape the urgency, like she needed to figure out how to do something meaningful with her life and be successful and make money *right now*.

"We'll love you no matter what you do," Leonor said.

Briani *really* needed to hear that from her mom. But she also needed to really *hear* it. "Nobody is telling you that you have to be this or that," she reminded herself. "Nobody will love you less if you're not a lawyer. God gave you the ability to write really well. You can use that."

Her grades came in. She'd finished with a 3.5 GPA, two As and two Bs. She'd fought for those marks—especially the 89 she'd gotten in International Politics. But if she was being honest, she felt disappointed.

She reminded herself, *First semester was tough and you survived!*

She reminded herself, *It's hard to prepare for something you'd never seen before. What did you know about college before you got there?*

Next semester, she was taking French, and the only thing she could say currently was, "*Oui, oui baguette.*"

She was kind of terrified, because college French wasn't going to be a dinky high school language class but complete immersion, the professor hitting you with grammar and pronunciation all at once.

What if French kept her out of law school?

What if Columbia kept her out of law school? Whereas some schools had grade inflation, everyone said Columbia had grade deflation. She was part of an Ivy League Facebook group where kids joked that Harvard was the toughest school to get into, but the easiest place to get straight As.

And yet the thought of complaining—or even worrying—about any of this made her feel totally ungrateful.

And then, suddenly, she knew what she had to do. It didn't exactly solve the conflict of happiness, meaning, and self-sufficiency. She wasn't even sure it would lessen her anxiety. Honestly, it might do the opposite. But that didn't matter. Briani now felt, deeply in her heart and her gut and her brain, that second semester she was going to apply for the *Columbia Daily Spectator*. No matter what.

She'd probably need a second job. But she'd make it work.

Her grades might suffer. But she'd make it work.

Her parents, despite their unflagging support, might wonder, *Is this the best idea?* She'd make it work.

And just like that, she'd wrestled her existential angst into submission. (For now, anyway.) Second semester opened before her like a vista of possibility. "I'm optimistic," she said. "I'm hopeful. I'm putting myself out there."

SECOND SEMESTER

JANUARY

HEADLINES: JANUARY 21–30

Columbia Daily Spectator: "Community Members See Long-Awaited Safety Improvements to Morningside Park in Aftermath of Majors' Death"

The Atlanta Journal-Constitution: The first case of a coronavirus person-to-person infection in the United States was confirmed by the Atlanta-based Centers for Disease Control and Prevention.

The Springfield News-Leader: According to DHSS, there have been no confirmed coronavirus infections in Missouri . . . The closest case to Missouri so far is one person in Arkansas who is being monitored by health officials there.

CONNER

The Triumphant Return

What was it about New York City points of entry? LaGuardia Airport probably tied with Port Authority Midtown Bus Terminal as the country's dankest, dirtiest, dingiest travel hub. And yet it didn't bother him. It seemed, somehow, appropriate.

Conner lugged his suitcases out of the terminal and into the frigid, exhaust-filled air of Queens. He should have gotten into the taxi line. Instead, he ended up with the livery drivers and hopped into one of the infamous, unregulated black cars. The cost of his ride to campus: $100.

On the upside, he walked into his dorm room in Carman to find . . . nobody. He still had no roommate. He was blissfully alone.

On the downside, there were a couple of dead roaches on the floor.

But, on the upside, he could finally do laundry and know his clothes wouldn't smell like mildew. Back home, the machine was kinda broken—something wrong with the belts—and the water just sat there, gross and fetid.

Also, on the upside, he'd gotten into an awesome American studies course on noir fiction. Sure, he'd be the only freshman in the seminar, and the final paper was 60 percent of his grade. But he was up to the challenge.

And other than that? Well, he was missing home. His first weekend back in New York, he spent so much time playing video games with his Missouri friends that he'd forgotten about Board Game Club. But his mom was doing better. Usually, when she started feeling bad, she'd wait until things spun off the rails and end up in ER. This time, though, she'd made a doctor's appointment to get her medication sorted. It was a big step.

BRIANI

The Interview

It was 6:00 p.m. and already dark, so maybe not the best time to be walking so close to Riverside Park. What happened to Tessa was still fresh in her mind, and the Riverside Church felt far from the campus hub. She texted a bunch of her friends where she was going and then texted again at the church door to let them know she'd arrived. If Briani was hired—if she didn't bomb this interview—she would be coming here at all hours.

She switched off *The Daily*, the *New York Times* podcast she'd been piping into her brain, and waited for the elevator to arrive. She'd applied to be a writer for *The Eye*, *Spec*'s long-form magazine. She needed to kill this.

The early weeks of second semester had been rough. Briani had gotten sick almost immediately after returning to campus in late January. It was some kind of cold/flu/sinus thing, and it knocked her out. Then there was school. After a blissful six-week break, the workload felt like being thrown headfirst into a freezing pool. French was as hard as she'd anticipated. University Writing, the mandatory freshman expository writing seminar, was a massive amount of reading in addition to the writing. She was digging Latin American Race Immigration and Ethnicity, but whoa, was that syllabus long. And let's not even talk about the marathon that was the second semester of Lit Hum: one hundred pages assigned the first week.

Finally, she'd been biting her nails over whether she'd be selected for the Presidential Global Fellowship, a program that would allow her to study abroad in Paris that summer, all expenses paid. In her application, she said she hoped to explore France's migrant experience amid the country's growing nationalism.

She was super excited.

But in the end, she didn't make the cut.

She felt deflated. She needed a win.

So now, here she was, twenty minutes early for her interview. And while it was generally good to be early, this felt weird early. She went through various interview scenarios. *Remember,* she thought, *you worked on yearbook. You have journalism experience. Just come as you are and show your enthusiasm. If we vibe, we vibe.*

Briani was called into the interview room to find *Spec*'s managing editor and the editor of *The Eye*: two women of color. This was encouraging. Also encouraging: *The Eye*'s editor gave Briani a huge smile. Less encouraging, the managing editor did not. There was something intimidating about her, like she didn't laugh a lot. What if she was put off by Briani's bubbly energy?

The editors welcomed her, then asked why she wanted to be on *Spec*.

"Before I came to Columbia," Briani said, "I romanticized what it would be like. But there's problems here. And the community deserves to know: not just the students, but the alumni and the people in Harlem." She paused, tried to gauge how this was going. At least *The Eye*'s editor was still smiling. "Writing things down signals that they're important," Briani said. "You're etching them into permanence."

The rest went by in a blur. They asked her to talk about a magazine article that stood out to her. Momentarily, she panicked. She hadn't known to prepare for this. But wait—there was that story about strip club hustlers, the one that became a movie with J.Lo. Where had she read that? Maybe *The Atlantic*? And how long ago was it? She remembered the movie better than the article. It would have to do.

"What J.Lo said at the end—it was profound," Briani told the women. "America is a strip club. We're all dancing and wanting attention, wanting praise."

And just like that, it was over.

We'll let you know, they said. Thanks for coming in.

FEBRUARY

HEADLINE: FEBRUARY 6

Columbia Daily Spectator: "Anti-Chinese Message Written in Butler as Anxiety Rises"

BRIANI

Cruise Ship

The elevators in John Jay were insanely slow, but fourteen flights of stairs? She'd rather wait in the line. So Briani stood in the lobby, waiting, scrolling through *BuzzFeed*. She clicked on the headline: "31 Tweets That Show What It's Like on the 'Coronavirus Cruise Ship'"

She vaguely remembered reading on New Year's Day about the virus that was spreading in Wuhan, China. But she hadn't thought much of it. China was so far away, and she'd never even heard of Wuhan. This cruise ship wasn't much closer. It was docked off the coast of Japan. It totally sucked for the people who were stuck there, but there were only 135 cases of coronavirus out of more than 2,500 people. And since everybody had been quarantined, it's not like the virus could spread. Also, there didn't appear to be that many Americans on board, so this wasn't really a threat to New York.

Briani reached the front of the queue and the elevator doors opened. By the time she got out again, she'd put the cruise ship out of her mind.

CONNER & JACKLYNN

Fire Signs

IN MISSOURI

Within a week of starting her second semester at OTC, Jacklynn had seriously improved her social life. She joined a group chat with some women in her psych class and bonded with her chemistry lab partner. Her two best friends at work had also started including her in their various friend-group outings: parties and hikes and hang outs. Honestly, it felt awesome.

But some things didn't change, like the anxiety that was constantly creeping up on her, tripping her up, pushing her into bottomless wells of doubt. It happened again on a Thursday night in February. Out of nowhere, an older male bartender lectured her about her emasculating sense of humor. In front of their coworkers! Jacklynn knew this was messed up, but she couldn't shake the fear that her colleagues didn't like her after all.

She arrived home in tears. She needed Conner to reassure her. She needed Conner to talk her down. She needed Conner to *be* there. But Conner wasn't there.

IN MANHATTAN

Resolved: You Can't Shit in the Same River Twice.

Another Thursday night, another meeting of the Philolexian Society. Each week, they debated a ridiculous resolution. Tonight's wasn't terribly inspiring. Still, Conner joined the roughly thirty people who'd come to a large meeting room in the student center to celebrate this bastardization of the ancient Greek philosopher Heraclitus. (The real phrase is, "No man ever steps in the same river twice.")

Conner was just happy to be here, soaking up the insane ceremony of it all. Club officers with titles like Censor, Scriba, and Moderator placed "sacred" objects on a table at the front of the room: a skull covered with member signatures, a Frisbee, a rubber ducky on a satin pillow, an Irish flag, Mr. Potato Head, and a gavel.

Sitting behind the table, the Moderator poured the contents of a flask into a stadium cup and took a big sip. A student in the audience stood up and requested that everyone Venmo her money for the after-party. A group of students vigorously debating D&D pulled out their phones to comply. In a few hours, most of the people in this room would head out to play beer pong.

Conner did not contribute to the fund. But he also had his phone out. Jacklynn was texting. She was upset. Again.

IN MISSOURI

Her social anxiety had appeared, full-blown, back in high school. When she was first afflicted, her friends didn't believe her. *How can you be in theater or speech and debate and be afraid? How can you lack confidence in yourself if you're willing to stand on a stage like that?* Jacklynn didn't have an answer. She was used to thinking of herself as an extrovert. The anxiety made her feel like a timid creature. That wasn't her!

At a friend's suggestion, she'd recently taken up astrology. Maybe she could discover more about herself, confront this anxiety head-on. Jacklynn was a Sagittarius, a fire sign. It was actually pretty accurate. Curious? Check. Generous? Check. Honest to a fault? Double check.

But fire signs also loved change, and she did not. Case in point: she'd been wanting to quit Big Whiskey's for a while now. There was just way too much workplace drama. But she hadn't. She doubted she would. Her childhood had left her craving stability. Once she'd gotten it, she wanted to keep it. Other kids moved across the state for school. Jacklynn had felt fine living at home and continuing to date the same guy. As she said on one occasion, "If it's not broke—or if it can be salvaged—then don't mess with it."

Jacklynn didn't want to be ruled by fear. But after her foray into astrology, she wasn't sure she wanted to be ruled by consistency, either.

IN MANHATTAN

Yes, she needed him frequently, but it wasn't like her need was disruptive. He could pay attention to Philo (a senior was talking about the made-up campus committee he ran called Committee of the Youth Who Are Corrupting *Me*, which somehow related to the river argument), while also helping his girlfriend through a crisis. It was simply multitasking. And a Philo meeting was more about the atmosphere, anyway. It was like an avant-garde play, where members tried to sound as dramatic and pompous as possible. The specifics weren't *that* important.

I'm sure it's not as bad as you think, Conner texted after Jacklynn explained what her colleague had said. Everything will be fine. It will blow over.

He watched the text dots appear on the screen, then disappear.

His attempts to console her never felt good enough. Like he was always saying the wrong thing. One time, her boss got angry because she was on her phone at work. And Conner's advice—don't be on your phone—seemed reasonable enough. An argument for cause and effect. But Jacklynn got pissed at him—just like she was pissed now.

Blowing over isn't the point, she texted.

What is *the point?* he wondered.

IN MISSOURI

She was relieved to discover that Conner (an Aries) was also a fire sign. This meant they were both stubborn, but also compatible. Of course, Conner (quite stubbornly) didn't believe in astrology. He made fun of her after she'd texted his mom for his exact time of birth. She knew he was trying to be playful, but it still hurt her feelings.

This was the thing about Conner. You couldn't just have an opinion or random belief about something. You needed an airtight case, like you were arguing for a Philo resolution but doing it in front of the Supreme Court.

Resolved: Astrology Isn't Just Bullshit.

Resolved: A Belief in Astrology Is Compatible with a Belief in God.

And while we're at it, resolved: God Exists.

She felt like one of them always had to win. Generally, that was Conner. Because Jacklynn didn't think about arguments like he did. What if some things *weren't* logical or consistent. Couldn't a river be both the same and different at the same time?

IN MANHATTAN

She considered him argumentative—he knew this. But he saw himself differently. Just because he often wanted to hear more on a claim or asked pointed questions didn't mean he was automatically rejecting it. But she always assumed he was acting in bad faith. She also accused him of being pretentious, like he thought only a simple person would believe in astrology. For him, astrology was kind of goofy, sure. But his mom had been into the hobby her whole life. To each his own.

Meanwhile, the Philo argument was ramping up. One of the members had even brought a copy of Heraclitus to the meeting and was reading aloud from the text. "No man ever steps in the same river twice, for it's not the same river and he's not the same man," he said. He slammed the book shut. Then he launched into an oration that somehow linked the "metaphysical fixity of death" with the movies *Caddyshack* and *The Goonies*.

Jacklynn was still writing. Conner waited for the next bomb to drop.

IN MISSOURI

Things between them were fine right now, pretty good, even. And sure, they bickered constantly. But hadn't they *always*? In any case, she was starting to sense the irony of the situation.

Conner picked up and left. He'd been incredibly brave. But he wasn't changing. Just because you went to Philo meetings didn't mean you were getting to know Philo members. For instance.

Meanwhile, she hadn't gone anywhere, but she was *moving*. Fighting through the anxiety and doubt, trying to build a new life for herself. She wanted him on those adventures, like whatever luring ocelots meant in real life. Did he want to go with her?

IN MANHATTAN

The argument began to escalate. Jacklynn dropped more doubt. Conner replied, knowing, even as he typed, that his responses were insufficient. Jacklynn grew increasingly angry and, frankly, started to become mean. Now her texts were littered with curses and insults. Conner knew he shouldn't take the bait, but he couldn't help himself. He began to curse and insult her back.

IN MISSOURI

Maybe fire signs were less compatible than she'd thought. Because wasn't this the obvious outcome when two people who felt deeply hurt were also deeply defensive?

IN MANHATTAN

He was so tired of doing this with her. But what was the alternative? He loved her and wanted to help her. He'd keep trying until he got it right. Their future was together. He rarely, if ever, questioned that.

BRIANI

Cassandra

It was Friday, February 14th, Valentine's Day, and Briani was waiting for the interminably slow John Jay elevator. Her Lit Hum class was taking a field trip to see the antiquities collection at the Metropolitan Museum of Art. All part of their work on Homer.

On her way out of the dorm, she was listening to yesterday's *New York Times Daily* podcast: "Fear, Fury and the Coronavirus." It was about a Chinese eye doctor in Wuhan who was punished for telling people about the virus. The government made him sign a document saying he'd spread false and illegal information. Then he caught the virus himself and died.

The elevator arrived and Briani stepped in.

How devastating! To think that some governments suppressed information like that. It reminded her of the Trojan princess Cassandra. In *The Iliad* she was cursed by the Gods: to utter prophecies that nobody believed.

Briani remembered that cruise ship she'd read about while waiting for another John Jay elevator. But the coronavirus was still mostly in China, which meant it wasn't a threat to the United States. Which meant it was only news, totally contained to the news apps on her iPhone.

By the time she stepped off the subway with her friends a while later, she'd forgotten about the podcast. She pulled some Trader Joe's hand sanitizer from her tote and spritzed it on. You never knew what germs were lurking in the train.

BRIANI

Trolled

The email from *Spec* dropped that same afternoon: Congrats for making it to the next round. According to the message, round two was that very evening at 7:00 p.m.

Maybe if she'd had a Valentine's date, if some guy had promised to shower her with gifts or a fancy dinner, she would have been annoyed. *That's bold of you, assuming we don't have plans tonight*, she thought. *But you're right . . .*

She returned to the Riverside Church that evening in her V Day attire: red sweater and red lipstick. She walked into the room where they'd held the open house last semester to find a ton of applicants. How many were competing for *The Eye*? How many were they going to hire? Did her competitors all want this as badly as she did? She assumed so. She assumed they were all crazy impressive, all super passionate. They were all Columbia students, after all. It was the upside and the downside to being at a school like this. The people were amazing, but because the people were amazing, the competition was intense.

The students vying for *The Eye* were told to gather in the magazine's office. Maybe ten of them plus the editors crowded in. The hopefuls were asked to sit down at the table, and Briani listened with growing anxiety as she was handed a test.

A TEST?!

Briani scanned the page. She had to identify thirty acronyms like MRC, KSA, URC, and (was this a joke?) LMFAO. Then she had to list the names of obscure administrators, like Assistant Vice President for Environmental Stewardship and the Assistant Vice President for Public Safety.

Was she really supposed to know this stuff?

And then a prompt: Write a pitch. On the spot. And include not just the idea for a story but an investigative question, the potential angle, critical sources, and why the piece was a fit for *The Eye*.

Around her, heads were down, hands furiously writing.

Briani took a breath. She could do this. She had a Mexican friend who didn't feel accepted by any of the Latinx or Mexican student organizations. She could pitch a story about identity on campus: Who defined identity, and what happened if you didn't fit the definition? It had an interesting conflict, was timely and relevant. She hoped the editors would agree.

Midway through, though, the timer went off. Briani dropped her pen. But before she could dwell on this, the editors were hustling them into another room, this one full of all the candidates. Maybe fifty people.

This was the second part of the test, the editors said, passing out folded pieces of paper.

Briani took hers and waited for the clock to start. Open your papers, the editors said. She did.

Written there it said *Welcome 144th Cohort of* Spectator *Trainees. Congratulations.*

Briani was stunned. She was hired?! Everybody was looking

around like, *What just happened*? Who knew that being trolled could feel this awesome!

The editors explained what would happen next: the weekly staff meetings, the profile and feature story she'd be writing during her training period, the work-study hours that would put her about $600 shy of the money she needed for her Student Contribution.

She was too excited to worry about it. Last semester she'd been afraid of the money, the time commitment, the rejection. Now she'd drummed up her courage. A new semester had begun.

BRIANI

Sorority

People said you had to go to at least one. A frat party that is. But Briani could do better: She'd attend two in the same night, just to give it an extra college try.

She wore a halter top, some black-and-white gingham pants, and her Picasso-inspired earrings. A friend did her eye makeup. One of the parties was themed Heaven and Hell. Or maybe Inferno? She couldn't remember, but Hell would have been accurate. Even sober, the experience was a hot, sweaty blur. All those bodies jammed together, air that felt like damp skin, the smell of beer, low-key weed, and a disgusting alcoholic concoction that everyone called jungle juice. A guy came up behind her and drunkenly slurred into her ear, "You're really pretty." Briani was too skeeved to respond. Luckily, one of her friends grabbed her by the arm and pulled her away. Had it been possible, she would have poured a bucket of that Trader Joe's sanitizer over her head.

But the thing about Saturday night was that there was always Sunday morning. And this Sunday morning meant an outing with Genevieve to see Jean-Michel Basquiat and Dorothea Lange at the Museum of Modern Art. They got in for free with their student IDs and wandered the echoing chambers in Converse sneakers (Briani) and patent-leather platforms (Genevieve), snapping photos with their manual cameras. Genevieve was taking a course; Briani was looking for a new landscape. Columbia's campus, at first so awe-inspiring, was starting to look like background. Remarkably, it had become normal.

Briani carried a cloth Madewell tote that said BIEN FAIT. Genevieve carried a leather tote, which her aunt had gifted her. It read BERNIE 2020.

They chatted about how much they loved Bernie, how they thought he was the only candidate who would actually remain true to his values if elected. They walked quietly, somberly among the photos of dust bowl migrants. They stopped in front of a Keith Haring and continued their never-ending conversation about parental expectations. Genevieve was starting to wonder if her mom had really pressured her to follow a practical path—or whether her mom had been supportive and *she*, Genevieve, was the one hyper-focused on responsibility.

"It's in my nature to want to please people," Briani said. "But that's not my job. Poli-sci and pre-law—is this what I want? Have I just convinced myself? And then there's journalism, which I love."

They entered the gift shop. Briani gushed over a black tote bag with smiley faces drawn in the aesthetic styles of famous artists, from Leonardo da Vinci to Andy Warhol. Underneath, it said HISTORY OF ART. She looked at the price tag. *Nope.* She moved on.

A minute later Genevieve appeared, holding two HISTORY OF ART totes and a receipt.

"You didn't!" Briani was dumbfounded. Her eyes filled with tears.

Genevieve smiled, made an excuse about how she'd just gotten her paycheck. And all at once, the girls melted together: their dark hair in each other's faces, their arms wrapped tightly. The new totes swung from their shoulders as their joy rose octave over octave into the air.

MARCH

HEADLINE: MARCH 1

The New York Times: "Coronavirus in N.Y.: Manhattan Woman Is First Confirmed Case in State"

HEADLINE: MARCH 4

Columbia Daily Spectator: "University Suspends Sponsored Overseas Travel, Asks Students to Prepare Return from Programs Abroad"

BRIANI & CONNER

March 6: Georgia or Georgia

They wished they had more time to participate in First-Generation, Low Income activities. There were plenty of options: QuestBridge; the First-Generation, Low Income Partnership, aka FLIP; the FLI Student Advisory Board; the weekly lunchtime FLI hang outs hosted by the office of Multicultural Affairs. There were FLI study breaks and FLI workshops. National conferences that convened FLI students from across the country. But for Briani and Conner, these activities were satellite planets, floating in their general orbit. Now and then, they touched down. Their classes, on the other hand, were gravity. *Spec* and Philo were their oxygen. Necessary to survive.

Even so, the first week of March, they attended an FLI Town Hall at the office of Multicultural Affairs. Conner arrived in a baseball cap that said BUC-EE'S, which he'd bought at a truck stop in Texas, and Converse sneakers that seemed to be disintegrating on his feet. He had other shoes, he said, but these were simply the most comfortable. Briani was casual, with athletic pants and her Madewell tote.

It was the first time they'd formally met and, to be honest, it was awkward. They smiled at each other, gave a half wave. For all they had in common—from their financial struggles, to their intermittent fish-out-of-water feelings, to their studiousness, to being the first in their families to attend college—their life experiences couldn't have been more different. And yet here they were together—on a campus, in a book—joined by some combination of circumstance, coincidence, and, if you asked Briani, fate.

After a series of introductions by student leaders and administrators, the fifteen or so town hall attendees were split into small groups and shuttled into ancillary conference rooms. "So," the student-moderator asked, "what are some of the concerns you have about being FLI at Columbia?"

The four students in Briani and Conner's group looked at each other. Nobody wanted to speak first, but somebody had to fill the silence. And so they began.

Problem: Financial aid either didn't understand the problems FLI students were having with their bills, or if they did, the officers didn't know how to solve them.

Problem: The Deans' Student Assistance Fund only covered certain things. Winter coats? Yes. Money to help a student when her family's home was flooded during a hurricane? No.

Problem: Academic departments had resources to help low-income students cover various costs, but professors either didn't know about these funds or their departments made students jump through hoops to get them. One student said her professor even paid out of pocket to help her get to a mandatory play.

Benefit: The FLI identity wasn't obvious, which meant most people couldn't tell you lacked money just by looking.

Problem: But nobody was going to be sensitive to your needs, because they didn't know you were poor. And looks could be deceiving. One young woman asked for an emergency meal swipe, offered to kids who were short on dining credit. The administrator took one look at her nice outfit—she was dressed for a job interview—and said she didn't need it.

Problem: The library, including the new FLI lending library, did not carry a lot of course texts. So if you couldn't afford to buy those books, what were you supposed to do?

Problem: A lot of students had already read the Lit Hum books in high school. This meant classes sometimes devolved into those students having inside baseball conversations with their professors. If you couldn't join in, you felt "behind" (these, Briani's air quotes). At the very least, it meant you had to work harder, which ate up more hours of the day, which meant less time to socialize or explore the city or do extracurriculars.

Problem: A lot of these extracurriculars were financially inaccessible. Like scuba diving, or snowboarding. It was partly why Conner liked Philo and Board Game Club. There were no applications, no financial expenditures, no airs.

Less a problem than an annoyance: Earlier that day, a kid in Briani's University Writing seminar was complaining that the coronavirus might cancel his spring break trip to Amsterdam. "I'd have to go home," he'd said, like this truly sucked. And Briani thought, "So sorry to hear that. My spring break plans are either Georgia or Georgia."

Less of a problem than a realization: Social capital was a real thing. An FLI student at the table said she was having trouble getting her service dog certified. When she mentioned this to a

215

classmate, the girl said, "Oh, my mom's a doctor. She could help," like of course the adults in your life had special connections or could work the system.

Problem: The guilt you felt when your parents tried to help you. Like the $50 that Leonor and José had put into Briani's account, because she hadn't yet been paid by *Spec*. Every time she logged on and saw the money sitting there, she felt angry. She didn't live at home anymore. She needed to be independent.

Problem: Yes, the FLI student advocates had convinced the university to give them subsidized subway cards, a lending library, and a food pantry. But Conner wondered whether these meetings were all that productive. "To be honest," he said, "the administration being not responsive in some specific areas is something I've heard over and over again. I think they know what issues they have. So the meetings are more signaling that they care."

HEADLINES: MARCH 7

The New York Times: "Coronavirus in N.Y.: Cuomo Declares State of Emergency"

The New York Post: "Coronavirus Puts NY College Students' Spring Break Trips on Hold"

Christian County Headliner News: "First Case of Covid-19 Virus Confirmed in Missouri"

March 8: Time-Sensitive Update on Covid-19

Dear fellow members of the Columbia community:

. . . because a member of our community has been quarantined as a result of exposure to the Coronavirus (COVID-19), we have decided to suspend classes on Monday and Tuesday

   . . . prepare to shift to remote classes for the remainder of the week.

   . . . does not mean that the University is shutting down

   . . . This action is intended to prevent the virus from spreading.

Sincerely,
Lee C. Bollinger
President, Columbia University

CONNER

March 9: Prelude to the Apocalypse

Conner woke up late Monday morning and lay in bed checking his email. Everything was changing by the second.

Classes were temporarily canceled.

Exams were now remote.

The semester would be pass/fail.

He couldn't complain. He no longer had to worry about Fro Sci wrecking his GPA. And sure, it was a little concerning that people were joking about the apocalypse, saying there'd be no more school after spring break. But Conner didn't believe that. Not really.

He wasn't supposed to leave campus for five more days. Now he wondered if he should get home sooner. There was a pandemic spreading, after all. He called his grandmother, who always covered his airfare, and she agreed that he should leave.

The next morning at 6:00 a.m., he flew out of New York City on a mostly empty plane. A lot of people at LaGuardia were masked, but Conner didn't have one. He wasn't super concerned. Almost nobody at Springfield-Branson was masked, either.

Conner had hoped to surprise his mom. He imagined how

delighted she'd be to suddenly see him on the doorstep five whole days early. But his grandparents didn't want to risk being infected by him, so they asked Stacey to pick him up.

Conner also hoped to surprise Jacklynn, but Stacey said, *I don't want you leaving the house.* And Conner didn't want to have a fight five minutes after getting home. So he FaceTimed Jacklynn instead, watching her face morph from confusion to excitement when she realized he was sitting in his Missouri bedroom.

BRIANI

March 10: Pandemic Bacchanal

When had the virus arrived—like, really arrived? It still didn't seem real. Sure, Briani had been following the news. Two days ago there were twenty-one cases in the city. Now there were sixty-nine.

But look out the window! With classes canceled, everyone was outside, lounging in the 64-degree weather, throwing Frisbees, and sipping iced coffees. Last night, kids had thrown "cancelation of class" parties. It was almost like Bacchanal—Columbia's spring fling—had come early. She'd heard so much about the event from upperclassmen and couldn't wait to experience it for herself. There was a rumor that Doja Cat was scheduled to perform.

Now people were saying Bacchanal might not happen.

Because one member of the Columbia community was exposed. One person! And because of that, they'd shut everything down for a week. That's how serious this was. Think, what one infected person could do to a community of ten thousand. Brooklyn had left, booked it out of there and returned home to Buffalo at the urging of her family.

On the other hand, Briani was pretty sure that NYU was still holding classes. Her brother's high school was still in session.

And weren't most young people who were catching Covid-19 mostly fine?

On a group chat, Briani's friends Leila and Elliot didn't have any more clarity than she did.

"I'm more worried about my grandparents," Leila said.

"I think there's a general feeling of unease," Elliot said. "But that's to be expected, given the press."

It was weird, Briani said, how some people were rushing to get away from the city, while others didn't seem concerned at all. Leila said people were still hooking up, which struck her as idiotic. But she and the others admitted they weren't exactly social distancing. They'd stopped shaking hands, but . . . they were still together in the dorms, way closer than six feet apart. They were still trying to figure out their comfort levels—and manage their parents' (much lower) comfort levels.

Leila's dad flat-out told her, "I don't want you taking the subway."

Leonor had issued Briani a list of instructions:

— *Be careful.*
— *Carry hand sanitizer.*
— *Wash your hands frequently.*
— *Use the sanitizer after you touch anything on the subway.*
— *Don't go on the subway.*
— *Maybe don't go to church.*
— *If you go to church, be mindful because people are close to you and you don't know if they are infected.*

Even so, the girls did not think the world was falling apart. "I'm hoping it'll pass and things will go back to normal," Briani said.

"I don't want to finish the semester at home," Leila said. "As long as we're allowed to be in the dorms, I will be. I plan on coming back when break is over."

HEADLINE: MARCH 11

The New York Times: "Coronavirus Has Become a Pandemic, W.H.O. Says"

MARCH 12: WWW.COLUMBIA.EDU

. . . all classes for the remainder of the semester will be conducted online. Students who are able to move out of undergraduate residence halls for the rest of the semester are encouraged to do so.

HEADLINE: MARCH 13

Christian County Headliner News: "OTC Shifts Courses Online for Rest of Semester"

. . . OTC Chancellor Hal Higdon sent out [a] message just moments before the Springfield-Greene County Health Department and Gov. Mike Parson announced that the second presumptive positive case of coronavirus in Missouri occurred in Springfield. The patient, a 20-year-old woman, is not part of the OTC community.

BRIANI

March 14: First Generation

Briani wasn't going home for spring break. She was simply going home. Which meant she now had to stuff all her belongings into just a few boxes, while also trying to pack a semester's worth of memories into just a couple of hours. She marveled at how everyone—which is to say, Twitter—was responding. Bring on the Covid Memes, Boomer Remover!

"It's so interesting how our generation is coping," Briani said. "College kids saying, 'Well, if I die, at least I die in California or Paris instead of Oklahoma'"

Genevieve, bless her heart, announced that she was taking Briani out for lunch. They walked down to Wu and Nussbaum on Broadway for avocado toast and overnight oats. Sitting there, definitely not socially distanced, they looked at pictures from first semester, laughing like old friends who'd known each other for years.

Afterward, they set out for Levain Bakery, Briani's favorite. It was located in Harlem, across Morningside Park. After what happened to Tessa, Leonor made it clear that her daughter was not to take that route. But it was broad daylight, and there were more police these days. So the girls strolled down the long escarpment steps, snapping pictures. At Levain they bought chocolate chip walnut cookies and took more pictures. On their way back, they stopped in the park to snap even more. The day was sunny, the buds just starting to pop on the hickories and maples. The air was sweet on her tongue, sugar dusted. It did not smell like sickness. Only later that night would she think about the many spring days ahead—days she would not be coming here. Only later did she consider what it meant for an entire city to shut down. The Met, closed. Broadway, dark. The dorms, empty.

Briani felt a pang for the seniors, who might not even get their commencement. But mostly, she felt a pang for herself. There was a beauty in experiencing something for the first time: her first spring in New York, her first Bacchanal. And of course, it sucked for all of them. Nobody in the Class of 2023 would be finishing their first year of college on campus. But as far as firsts went, wasn't Briani's pain a little deeper?

Because this wasn't just her personal first.

It was her family's first, too.

She remembered high school graduation, how a lot of kids were like, Just give me that diploma. But when Briani crossed that stage, she wasn't simply doing it for herself. It was the fruition of José and Leonor's toil.

What she did think, at the park, with Genevieve, was, *If I had known we'd be leaving like this, I wouldn't have spent the last couple of weeks in the library.*

It was time to get back to the dorm. Titi Jackie was coming to collect Briani's boxes and Genevieve had her work shift downtown.

They finished their cookies, licked the chocolate from their fingers, tossed the wrappers in the trash.

The next morning at 5:00 a.m., after four hours of fitful sleep, Briani woke up in her dorm room for the last time. Her room was fully packed. She thought back to the previous night: the lost moving bin, her frantic search to retrieve it, the guilty apology from her floormate. Honestly, it felt like a dream. She was leaving campus. Hadn't she only just arrived?

Genevieve came by to see her off. Standing outside the dorm in the coolish March morning, she handed Briani a card and a chocolate bar. It was 75 percent cacao, the fancy stuff. The thought her friend put into even the smallest action never ceased to amaze Briani. It buoyed her.

Later, she would read the card.

Dear Briani,

If someone were to tell me last summer that my closest friend at college would be from Georgia, I probably would have laughed and said "sure." . . . There's a kindness and empathy that you possess that I've so rarely seen in other people . . . I truly do not know how I would have gotten through this semester without you . . . Thank you for loving me unconditionally . . .

Love, Genevieve

But for now, they hugged, tight. Then they walked, side by side, down College Walk under the bruise-blue sky.

At the Broadway and 116th Street subway stop, Briani asked Genevieve to watch her suitcase for just a second while she ran down the stairs and refilled her MTA card. She was sure she'd be back on campus before long, and she didn't want to be caught without the fare.

JACKLYNN

Social Distancing

Here's what happened:

— *By the middle of March, Jacklynn's anxiety attacks were few and far between.*

— *She now had a big group of friends—a first, since she'd spent her last two years of high school almost exclusively with Conner,*

— *She was reaching out to make plans instead of waiting for the phone to ring.*

— *She was getting into the groove of second semester.*

— *A global pandemic arrived and school went remote.*

She wasn't supposed to be going out, but it was hard to take the situation seriously. She didn't know anybody who was sick. And her best friend only lived two minutes away, so what was the harm of getting together? It wasn't like she was traveling across the state or going to massive parties. She'd meet up with a few friends to go on a hike, or grab food. How could this be contributing to any kind of spread? It just seemed impossible.

Jacklynn was also struggling to take classes seriously. Now that everything was virtual—and pass/fail—it all seemed like pretend. Stockpiling resources in the world of *Minecraft* had more urgency than her psychology paper. Which meant she'd been procrastinating even more than usual: done heaps of laundry and redecorated her room.

Maybe she was depressed?

She tried to pay attention to her lectures, but it all sounded like background noise. One of her OTC friends said that her class was performing so badly, the instructor had resorted to handing out better grades—her friend's D had magically upgraded to a C.

A few times Jacklynn considered just giving up on the semester. But the perfectionist, long-term planner in her knew that would be a terrible mistake.

Honestly, her classes were not her top concern. She was more worried about Conner—and their relationship. At first, she'd been thrilled to have him home for the semester. Finally, they could see each other, be with each other. She even took off work his first week back. But everything quickly went from excited anticipation to constant disappointment. She and Conner chatted, FaceTimed, and played *Minecraft* together, but he was barely allowed to come over. He might as well have been in New York.

She understood he was under a lot of pressure. His grandparents were calling all the time, telling him not to leave the house. Stacey wasn't taking her medication. Conner didn't talk about that much, but he'd mentioned his mom's panic attacks a couple of times. Jacklynn was trying to be understanding. But it was really hard: knowing your boyfriend was so close and you couldn't even touch him.

CONNER

Bittersweet

It was a quandary, for sure. What did you do when you'd already left (for break) and then school announced that you had to leave (for good)? Conner's dorm room was exactly as he'd left it, minus the clothes he'd packed for a week at home.

Student housing gave him the number for a moving company that would pack and store his belongings. But he'd reached out, what, a week ago? And he hadn't heard anything. Meanwhile, the school was saying all rooms needed to be emptied by March 17th. And then what? Would the school really throw out the contents of fully furnished rooms? He thought about the record player his grandfather had gotten him for Christmas and his camera. His second-semester course books were still there. (He hoped he could find the material online, because he couldn't afford to buy duplicates.) His clothes were still there and his winter coat. He'd only brought one pair of shoes home, but at least they weren't the pair full of holes. "I made the right decision there!" he said.

He worried, too, about his knickknacks. They were sentimental to him. Even if they were packed up in time, would his figurines hold up in storage? He missed looking at the lion figurine he and Jacklynn had bought for under a dollar at Walmart and the teacups he'd bought in Chinatown first semester.

It was weird to be at home, but also to be without the trappings of home he'd taken to school to make New York more homelike.

Did he want to spend money to have any of this stuff shipped back? He couldn't justify it. The school said students could apply for up to $500 in financial aid to cover move-out costs. Conner received the maximum. But then the bursar extracted $500 from his account for other expenses. Storage was going to cost at least $400.

"You would think they'd be able to leave my items in a room that is closed off, sealed, no lights on, and just leave that room alone," he said. "I wouldn't think that would cost them money. But apparently it does."

Logistics aside, the situation was bittersweet. On the sweet side: Home was familiar. At night, he'd have dinner with his brother and his mom, while watching *Supernatural* on the living room couch. His friends were a short drive away even if he didn't see them much. He was managing to visit Jacklynn occasionally.

On the bitter side: his internet connectivity was atrocious. It often dropped out, interrupting his Zoom classes. He'd given his professors a heads-up, and (on the sweet side) they seemed understanding.

But on the bitter side, there was no Philo, no Board Game Club. He even missed his dorm room, now that it was really his.

On the bitter side: the situation at home was stressful. His mom was paranoid. Without any real justification, she thought she'd contracted Covid. She'd made vague references about the government being responsible for the virus. Conner had heard crazier things from her, but he wondered if she needed medical attention. The hospitals didn't want people coming in, though.

So Conner hunkered down and didn't argue when Stacey told him not to leave the house. At least (on the sweet side) Ayden was having a ball with school being canceled, playing video games all day and living on ramen and doughnuts.

On the bitter side: the growing global pandemic. Conner wasn't worried about his own health—he was only nineteen—but what if he spread the virus? He felt a little reckless every time he left the house. His grandparents were in their sixties; Jacklynn's mom was high-risk, as was his friend Micayla.

Meanwhile, Jacklynn was out hiking with her friends. And then she'd get upset when he said he couldn't come over. It bothered him, because he was just trying to be responsible, to keep everybody in his life safe.

APRIL

HEADLINE: APRIL 5

St. Louis Post-Dispatch: "Governor Orders All of Missouri to Stay Home to Help Slow Spread of Virus"

Gov. Mike Parson put all Missouri residents under a stay-at-home order Friday, ending days of frustration for critics who said he should have taken the action weeks ago to help curb the spread of COVID-19.

JACKLYNN

Ghosting

And just like that, everything began to disappear. The products from the shelves. Jacklynn's boyfriend from her life. Her father from the world.

She and Sherry went to Walmart, because their fridge was nearly empty, and their shelves were looking bare. Soon they'd be relying on Kleenex in the bathroom. But at Walmart the shelves were equally bare. It was odd how the run on necessities pointed to hysteria, yet nobody was masked.

Inside the store, people took one look at Jacklynn and Sherry's masks and started to give them looks: *What's wrong with you? Are you sick?* Meanwhile, Jacklynn was keeping her breaths shallow, trying to touch as few things as possible—not her clothes, not her face, not her hair. Later, back at home, she and Sherry scrubbed their hands raw. Usually, they reused plastic shopping bags, but this time, they swallowed their environmental concerns and tossed them.

"You never know where it is or what it's on," Jacklynn said.

"And if I'm a carrier . . ." Sherry had some serious lung issues. She'd said "flat-out" to Jacklynn, *If I get this, I will not survive it.*

Jacklynn felt ashamed by how cavalier she'd been even a week ago. Now she was terrified.

It was her aunt's sixty-fifth birthday, and her family arranged a ten-car parade. After Jacklynn and Sherry had pulled past, honking their horn and waving signs, they headed across the highway to Conner's street. Jacklynn had barely seen Conner since he returned to Missouri. Now she vibrated with anticipation as her mom parked the car.

Jacklynn bathed herself in Germ-X and got out. Conner came through the front door, smiling, his cheeks red. He smelled fresh from the shower, and for a minute, they just stood in the front yard hugging. It was a relief to be close to him after so much distance. But it was fleeting, maybe ten minutes. Her mom was waiting in the car, and it was impossible to know what was safe.

A little later, as they rushed along the highway heading back to Ozark, Jacklynn thought about saying goodbye to Conner the night before he flew to New York.

That night, they'd stood outside her front door holding each other.

That night, he'd been the one driving away.

That night, she'd been excited for him, despite her tears.

Now she was the one driving off. She felt empty.

Maybe the world would have hung together, had her sister not called that very evening with news about their dad. Jacklynn knew that he'd been in the hospital for a few weeks, after collapsing outside the Salvation Army in Springfield. Now, Crystal said, the doctors realized he'd had multiple strokes. He couldn't move his limbs. He was barely responsive. He didn't recognize people. There was fluid in his lungs.

"He's given up," Crystal said. "He might have weeks, but more likely, days."

She said that because of Covid restrictions, family would not be able to visit until the very end.

Jacklynn was seized with fear. Suddenly, it seemed possible that she could lose both her parents—one was high-risk for Covid complications and one was on his deathbed. She was starting to realize that she hadn't really dealt with the loss of her dad five years before. And now she was going to lose him again, this time for good.

That night, Jacklynn sat awake in her room, worrying over a five-year mountain of unresolved feelings. Without paying it much attention, she'd let it grow taller and deeper until she stood beneath it, small in its shadow. She and Conner were on FaceTime together; he was doing homework and she was playing *Minecraft*. But soon, the emotion felt too big. She muted herself and began sing-crying to "I'm Already There," by Lonestar, a country song she and her dad used to listen to.

She was still up, worrying, when the sun began to rise. When she finally heard her mother stirring, she went into Sherry's room and cried.

BRIANI

Jell-O Time

Briani called it Jell-O Time, how they were stuck, suspended as though inside a bubble. During class, even over Zoom, Briani might forget that she wasn't on campus. But then she'd look up, see the poster of New York City on her bedroom wall, and remember where she was and why.

Thank God, she had her cousin Alberto. His dad was an NYPD sergeant who was now spending his days patrolling the siren-filled streets of Manhattan. The family decided Alberto would be safer in Georgia. It was a trade-off for sure. Under the leadership of Governor Kemp (the same anti-immigrant politician that her friend Maria had served at UGA's stadium), Georgia had reluctantly mandated shelter in place. Masks were few and far between.

Briani had Maia, too. But the friends had only met up a couple of times to walk their dogs. They were trying to be responsible.

Still, after a few cooped-up weeks, they had to get out. They needed an adventure.

Which meant visiting not one but *two* grocery stores.

They stood in Briani's driveway jockeying for shotgun and trying to decide whether to hit up Trader Joe's or Whole Foods first. They made sure they had their masks—Maia's was the kind you wore to bust through drywall and Briani's and Alberto's were maternity-ward yellow.

They climbed into the car. "Ooh, it smells nice!" Briani said. "I haven't driven for so long." She started the car and suddenly a male voice blasted over the speakers. The three friends were startled, then burst out laughing. "It connected to my brother's phone!" Briani announced. "He's on with his girlfriend. Call ended! Sorry, Joseph. He'll be so mad." She pulled onto the road.

Driving along, they extolled the virtues of TJ's, namely that it was cheap and carried literally everything. "Back home," Briani said, then stopped short. "I'm referring to New York as home! Well, there, I'd walk to Ninety-Third Street. The suburbs are not the same."

They talked about how their families were coping. If Leonor and José were stressed out, they didn't show it. Takeout was popular, and people were ordering like six margaritas at a time. But she hated that her parents spent every day around strangers. "It's our situation," she said. "It's how it has to be."

At night, they'd leave their shoes in the garage and immediately head to the shower. And though they wore masks, a lot of their customers didn't. José still had occasional pain from his bout of shingles back in the fall. Briani worried he was at increased risk for Covid.

Alberto said his dad was exposed to people constantly. The only consolation—if you could even call it that—was a reduction in his hours and the moratorium on overtime. Alberto had been reaching out to Cornell regularly to ask for help with the semester's tuition, but he couldn't get a straight response. (Eventually, the school would give him a refund for his housing costs.) Maia's mom was a teacher and plenty stressed running class remotely. But at least she was home.

"This virus shows the inequality in America," Briani said. "What's wrong with the health-care system, how people have to go to work because it's their only source of income." She said she felt for Tom Hanks, who recently announced that he'd contracted Covid. "He's older, but he's so rich. He can afford to quarantine in his mansion and get treatment."

Maia said that according to Twitter, you could find out if you were sick by coughing on a celebrity. "Because they can get tested," she said. "My friends with more money, they think this won't affect them."

Briani said she'd read an article about two classmates—one was quarantined in her family's fancy summer home while the other spent every day working in her mom's food truck. She said Zoom provided an interesting glimpse into other people's lives. "We're all in the same class, but damn your house looks nice," she said. "To me, big, big windows means money. It makes me think, Are y'all loaded?"

Briani logged on from her bedroom. It was a decent bedroom, nothing to be embarrassed about, nothing to be impressed by. Still, she preferred to put up memes as her background—a *SpongeBob* theme or *The Office*. A friend in Lit Hum had put up *Minecraft* bees, which had Briani laughing so hard. But then someone put up a background of their Lit Hum classroom on campus. After that, Briani said, she didn't feel much like laughing.

BRIANI

Housing Crisis

Every day brought a lesson in relativity. In high school, Briani had assumed her family was middle class. Then she got to Columbia and realized she was low income. Now the pandemic was showing her a whole new spectrum within low income. For example, there were people who could go home and people who couldn't.

On April 28th, the university sent a message to students saying that anyone who absolutely needed to remain in the dorms for the summer would be assessed $45 a day for at least some period of time. There were kids who could not go home because their home lives were unsafe or unstable for any number of reasons. Or because they had no home to go to. But how were these kids, especially, supposed to afford $45 a day?

Briani's editor at *The Eye* handed the assignment to her and another trainee. She was not prepared for this. Her previous story had been about how professors were adapting to Zoom. Now, all of a sudden, she was responsible for an investigative feature. It was, frankly, insane.

Her editor didn't exactly throw Briani into the deep end. She told Briani about a student organization called Columbia People's

Covid Response who had mobilized to demand a more equitable pandemic response from the administration. She'd even passed along Instagram handles of students involved with the group. Briani took to social and then started making calls.

Her first few days of reporting were informative. She learned that not all international students were wealthy, as she'd previously thought. In fact, some of them weren't sure how to get home but didn't have the money to stay in the city. She interviewed a low-income student who described how lonely and sad the nearly empty campus was—and this broke Briani's heart—how that isolation was preferable to the student's home life.

Every time she got on the phone with a source, she couldn't help but compare their circumstances to her own. *I have a home. My parents are here for me.* She was also stressed. For a week straight, her phone was glued to her body. Student after student lobbed accusations against the university. They used words like *eviction*. They were angry and scared.

And Briani took it all in. She spent hours transcribing interviews. She fielded requests from students whom she knew would be perfect sources but who demanded anonymity. She would have happily granted anonymity to anyone who asked. But her managing editor, Eve, said people needed a really good reason to omit their name or they couldn't participate.

And then in the back of her mind was a steady drumbeat of fear. She, Briani Netzahuatl—freshman, first-generation college student, and hefty financial aid recipient—was taking on the entire freaking university. Yes, she wanted to speak truth to power. She just hadn't expected it to happen so soon.

Because what if she got something wrong? In high school,

when she'd done some reporting for the yearbook, the vibe was pretty much, *If you wrote it, it must be right . . . right?*

Wrong.

She was now going up against a more than two-hundred-year-old institution—her dream school, no less—for its treatment of vulnerable students during a global pandemic. Anything that followed her byline was her responsibility. That was terrifying.

Another thing she hadn't considered when she joined *Spec* was the emotional toll of reporting such intense stories. For a week, she was at it day and night. Mentally and physically drained by the interviewing, transcribing, and writing. Emotionally drained hearing the fear in students' voices. Which put a big question mark beside that issue of impartiality.

Because she needed to get her facts straight.

But she also needed to keep her heart straight.

Her sources were real students, some of them facing homelessness. The university needed to be accountable. There was a right response and a wrong one. Right: Help vulnerable students. Wrong: Charge them money to live on campus.

How could she feel this way and be unbiased?

She hadn't yet talked to anyone from the administration; doing so required multiple approvals. And though she was prepared to listen, she doubted they'd be able to persuade her that the daily assessment was fair.

And so, she made a decision, which maybe wasn't the professional, objective journalistic decision but felt like the *right* decision: She was going to be an ally.

As she said later, "Somebody owed these students an explanation. So when I talked to them, I said, 'I'm more than just here for your story. I want you to know that I support you. I want to make you heard.'"

Then, in the middle of her reporting, Columbia released a statement: The school would now provide free summer housing for vulnerable students.

And just like that, this story, which Briani had been living and breathing 24/7, was moot.

She was too exhausted to be angry. She thought, *At the very least, these students get to stay on campus. Yeah, we put in all this work, but if my sources are okay, that's what matters.*

And she'd learned a lot. About how to be a journalist but also what kind of journalist she *wanted* to be. There was a future for her at *Spec*, but investigative reporter wasn't it.

MAY

HEADLINES

MAY 1

The Atlanta Journal-Constitution: "Georgia Governor Ends Stay-at-Home Order, Effect of Coronavirus 'Minimal' for Most, Governor Says"

MAY 4

KFVS12: "Mo. Stay-at-Home Order Expires"

Governor Mike Parson said citizens may start returning to economic and social activities, but must adhere to social distancing requirements, including maintaining 6 feet of space between individuals in most cases. There are currently no limitations on social gatherings.

JACKLYNN

Bedside Manner

Her father was 6'2" and a solid man with black hair. Now, lying in the hospital bed, his body was skeletal. His hair and skin were gray. He already looked dead. Jacklynn spent the day in his hospice room with her mom, her two sisters, and her brother-in-law. For hours, they sat, laughing and crying and sharing stories over her dad's still-breathing but unresponsive body. Jacklynn struggled to keep it together, but she was dealing better than her mom and sisters. Even her brother-in-law, Jake, had lost it, and he didn't even like Jacklynn's dad.

Jake retold the story about when he'd asked for Crystal's hand in marriage. And the first thing their dad said was, *Are you circumcised?* Nobody understood why Kelly cared so much. But his fixation on it totally overshadowed Jake's happiness.

Karma is a funny thing, though. Jacklynn's dad hated cats, and there was a portrait of a cat right above his hospice bed. So Jake took a photo of the scene—the hospital bed and the cat art—and said, "This is me getting back at you for what you said to me."

Then Jake removed the cat picture from the wall and hid it behind the dresser as a sign of respect.

Later, when Jacklynn relayed this story to Conner, he listened thoughtfully and said, "I know how important that relationship was for all of you, regardless of what happened between you and your dad."

It was exactly what she needed to hear.

Jacklynn's mom and oldest sister took turns holding Kelly's arms. She mostly hung back. But when her family went out to smoke, she approached the bedside and talked to her dad, tried to say some of the things she'd been unable to say for the last five years.

That evening, around 8:00 p.m., surrounded by his family, he passed away.

Later that night, back at home, Jacklynn was making a cheese quesadilla while FaceTiming Conner. She'd been at the hospital for twelve hours and was starving. "At least I hope my dad gets to be in heaven with his family," she said. Conner replied the only way he knew how, with reason. "I understand why that's comforting to think about," he told her. But that, he said, didn't make it true.

This was not what she needed to hear.

She took the quesadilla out of the microwave. She was too tired and sad to argue.

CONNER & JACKLYNN

Comfort Food

At 12:30 p.m., Conner arrived at Jacklynn's house with a personal pizza and two slices of cake. Jacklynn hadn't explicitly asked for pizza; she'd simply noticed that you could order pizza to her father's hospice facility and mentioned to Conner that it looked good. But when she said that, "I knew what I had to do," Conner said. The cake was a bonus, though sadly, by the time he arrived at the tea shop, they were down to just coffee mint (which he knew Jacklynn didn't like) and lemon (which was okay but not as good as the red velvet). "But cake," he concluded, "was better than no cake."

Conner sometimes did this sweet thing for Jacklynn: driving over to her house and coming into her room to wake her up. But the food was extra TLC. When Conner arrived, Jacklynn stumbled out of bed and went downstairs to unlock the door. "The reason I'm not more excited to see you," she said, "is that I was just dreaming you were in my house."

"I've already worn out my welcome," Conner said, and pulled her in for a hug.

In the late afternoon, she and Conner sat side by side on the couch in Jacklynn's living room. They looked tired, a bit disheveled. Conner needed a haircut. He'd stopped shaving regularly. Jacklynn's eyes were red. She wore an oversized *Goonies* T-shirt. Behind them hung an enormous painting, a pastoral scene with farmhouses and a little church. This was obviously not how the two of them had planned to celebrate the end of state quarantine. But they would take what they could get. Conner was still feeling a lot of pressure to stay home. His mom's need for the family to shelter in place was a lot stronger than the governor's.

"She's been coming into my room every five to ten minutes and asking if I'm okay," he said.

"When we're on the phone and she swings the door open, it even scares me," Jacklynn admitted.

"She's worried about getting the car relicensed. She thinks my grandparents on my father's side are out to get her. She thinks there's something wrong with the tires on my car. She's been having issues sleeping and with her medication. She's out, and she hasn't gotten it refilled. Last night, she slept on the floor outside Ayden and my rooms. I'm going to have to leave sometimes to visit you, but it's not easy."

"She hates me," Jacklynn said.

"She doesn't hate you," Conner said. "She's just a nervous wreck."

Jacklynn sighed. Neither option was any good. Honestly, nothing was any good right now. And that wasn't even counting her four days of finals. Oh, and the terror that school might be remote in the fall.

"If we didn't go back, I'd been here next Halloween," Conner said, trying to cheer her up.

"And Thanksgiving." Jacklynn smiled thinking about it. "And Christmas."

"I'd already be here for those," Conner said.

Jacklynn rolled her eyes. "And my birthday."

Conner shrugged. "I do enjoy spending time with you, I guess."

Jacklynn nudged him. "Shut up," she said.

BRIANI

Lasts

On the last day of class, Briani's Lit Hum instructor said, "Look, guys, coronavirus upended everybody's lives. This final isn't necessarily a priority for you all, nor should it be."

She said, "I'll do whatever I can to make sure you get something out of this. So we'll have an interview instead of a test."

She said, "You can talk to me about what you learned, what moved you."

Briani logged off Zoom and, just like that, it was over. Her freshman year at Columbia University. Or, more accurately, her freshman year at Columbia University conducted from a laptop in Lawrenceville, Georgia.

She'd imagined walking out of that seminar room for the last time, heading to a picnic with her classmates. She was a romantic like that. But here she sat, alone in her childhood bedroom, looking at a poster of New York City. No friends, nothing but the sounds of suburbia, some birds, maybe a lawn mower. It wasn't supposed to end like this.

A few days later, Briani sat for her Lit Hum interview. She told her instructor, "You made me feel safe enough that I could venture out of myself and navigate this part of my life. You made what could have been so scary and alienating something that made me embrace Columbia."

Briani finished speaking and watched in shock and amazement as her professor began to cry, right there on the screen.

To. Be. Done. She was exhausted. She was happy. She was grateful. It was like drinking a cold glass of water after a long day in the sun. Satisfaction. Nothing could prepare you for what this year was going to be. Not your parents, not your teachers, not your friends. For the first time in her life, she'd been truly alone, surrounded by strangers. And in New York City.

She'd lived in New York City!

There was still so much she didn't know. So much she hadn't experienced. Like, she only knew how to get around on the 1 Train.

But she knew how to get around on the 1 Train!

There was no denying it: Briani called Columbia home now.

From: James J. Valentini
Date: Fri, May 15, 2020, at 6:45 p.m.
Subject: Dean's Update | Summer and Fall

Dear Students,
Congratulations on completing this historic semester

at Columbia College . . . Typically, the end of finals leads to shared celebratory moments and excitement for summer plans. I recognize that this summer will be different from what you expected, however I encourage you to . . . discover new ways to view the summer and make it as rewarding as possible.

／. . . The College, which is 266 years old, has survived countless challenges throughout our history; we will continue to uphold our mission to cultivate critical and flexible thinkers and active citizens who marry their classroom learning with real world challenges . . .

Roar, Lion(s), Roar!
James J. Valentini
Dean of Columbia College and
Vice President for Undergraduate Student Life

SUMMER 2020

MAY / JUNE

CONNER & JACKLYNN

The Last Good Day

It was supposed to rain, but the sky was clear. A perfect early summer day. So they decided to go fishing. They dressed for the occasion: Conner in a green fish-patterned bathing suit and Jacklynn in a magenta T-shirt featuring a cartoon pelican. They could pretend they weren't in landlocked Missouri but somewhere farther away and much more exotic. Florida or the Caribbean.

It had been two weeks since her father's funeral. Conner had attended and felt uncomfortable, because the forty or so people in attendance weren't wearing masks. But he didn't say anything. He didn't want to start a fight or do anything that might upset Jacklynn.

It was the right decision. They'd been seeing each other more since her dad died. They'd been fighting less.

On fishing day, Conner picked her up. They drove to the gas station to secure the licenses and then to Walmart to gather supplies. Conner already had a pole, hooks, and weights. But they needed bait. He'd heard hot dogs worked well, but the cans of Vienna sausages were cheaper, so why not? He threw in a multitool for good measure. Jacklynn bought Conner a hammock, because everyone needed a decent hammock.

Their destination was Lake Springfield, a 318-acre man-made lake, which had been built as a cooling reservoir for a now-decommissioned power plant. It was a popular recreation spot, though neither Jacklynn nor Conner trusted the water. "Very toxic," was how Jacklynn described it.

They walked onto one of the piers, lugging beach chairs, and set up. The water looked refreshing, clean even, with the sun glinting off the surface. Conner fastened the bobber and weights to the hook, then showed Jacklynn how to cast the line. He popped open the can of sausages and speared a hunk of meat. But when the sausage hit the water, it began to disintegrate, small pieces of floating pork. It looked like cat puke. They tried again. And again. Every time, the sausage crumbled.

Finally, Jacklynn just stuck an entire sausage on the line and cast it into the water. But when she reeled it in, she discovered that the sausage was gone . . . along with the hook. They looked at each other and groaned. They started to laugh.

"Can you get me another hook?" Jacklynn asked.

"That was my only one," Conner said.

"Of course it was," Jacklynn said. But she was teasing. She wasn't really annoyed. She went into problem-solving mode, pulling the pop-top off the sausage can and using Conner's new multi-tool to make an impromptu hook. He looked up, saw what she'd done, and started laughing. The hook looked ridiculous. "I thought about doing that," he said. "But I didn't know if it would work." They laughed some more, and Jacklynn cast the line.

And for the first time in weeks, with the sun on her arms and the water lapping, Jacklynn felt peaceful, tranquil even. They did not catch any fish, but that was all right. The water was too toxic to eat them, anyway.

HEADLINES

May 26

The New York Times: "'I Can't Breathe': 4 Minneapolis Police Officers Fired After Black Man Dies in Custody"

May 26

The New York Times: "Bystander Videos of George Floyd and Others Are Policing the Police"

The initial police account of the death of a Minneapolis man did not mention that an officer's knee pinned him to the ground. "Please, I can't breathe," he said.

May 28

The New York Times: "Protests Continue to Rage After Death of George Floyd"

BRIANI & ALBERTO

How You Look Vs. Who You Are

Briani could not bring herself to watch the killing of George Floyd by police officers on May 25th. But she didn't need to watch this Black man die to know that it was murder. She was angry and the anger exhausted her. Just the other day, she and Maia had been talking about Ahmaud Arbery, who'd been gunned down by white residents while jogging in his Georgia town, and Breonna Taylor, who'd been gunned down by police in her Kentucky apartment.

And now George Floyd.

This, just as life was creeping toward—not normalcy but a new, maybe livable, kind of normal.

In recent weeks, she and Maia had been thrifting once. She'd also gone to the park and tried to avoid people without masks. (It wasn't easy; almost everyone was maskless.) She'd been looking for remote jobs, because Columbia, unlike Barnard, hadn't waived upcoming student fees.

But the gale-force wind that was George Floyd's murder swept these worries away. She needed to do something, but what?

She donated what little money she could spare to bail funds.

She checked on Maia and Genevieve. Opened her heart to their pain.

She fumed over the Insta pictures of rich kids out at dinner. (And felt a little vindicated reading some of the comments: *Open your purse, sis.*)

She and Maia analyzed the outpouring of support versus "support." The brands who put up black squares because they were afraid BIPOC would stop buying their stuff; the Black Lives Matter ads on Netflix; classmates from their high school who'd never seemed to care before suddenly calling out racism on the internet.

She argued with (okay, maybe screamed at) her mom about what was happening in the streets.

ALBERTO

It was midnight and a day or two into the protests when he finally got ahold of his dad. His father was patrolling, once again working full-time. Alberto had seen the news footage—peaceful marchers met with rubber bullets and tear gas. But he felt confident that his dad was doing the right thing. As far as he could tell, his father saw himself as a protector, not a rash responder. Certainly not instigator. His dad believed the police should not profile, should not stop and frisk, should not hurt innocents. His dad believed the protesters were not agents of chaos. That was a myth.

BRIANI

Her mom absolutely did not want her going to the Atlanta protests. Briani said Leonor was worried about Covid. But that wasn't all. Because her mom was getting all of her information about Black Lives Matter from Fox News. And so, she believed many of the protesters were looting and rioting.

Briani tried to explain that the reverse was true: looters and rioters were using the protests as cover to break the law.

Leonor said her brother was a police officer.

Briani said the protests weren't about whether any one cop was good or bad. They were about the entire system. She begged her mom to watch the raw footage—what the police were doing to peaceful marchers. If her mom could just see those, she thought, she might understand why people were so angry.

But Leonor wouldn't budge.

ALBERTO

His dad was a man of color who saw the pain that other people of color experienced. He knew that Black and low-income communities feared law enforcement. He told Alberto that when patrolling the Grand Concourse in the Bronx, he was professional and respectful. He felt outrage after what happened to George Floyd. But it upset him to see the police gaining an even worse reputation.

Alberto said that reputation existed for a reason.

Alberto's dad said he understood. He'd seen the profiling, the unjust treatment. But he was torn. Law enforcement was there to help. Men like him were supposed to be servants of the people. He carried himself a certain way on the job to make sure everybody knew that.

BRIANI & ALBERTO

They were brown, not Black. They understood this. They knew that where you sat on the color spectrum impacted how other people saw you. Colorism was real. So was gender bias.

And how did these things influence perception?

Briani was dark but a female.

Alberto was lighter but a male.

Who got a leg up or a leg down?

The fact that they even had to think about this was really screwed up. At the end of the day, being brown meant they did not feel safe around police officers. It didn't matter that they were related to one. As Briani pointed out, when she and her cousin were out in the world alone, law enforcement saw how they looked, not who they were. Son, niece, college students. *Ivy League* college students. Didn't matter. What did? Brown.

Alberto said he tensed up whenever he noticed a squad car on the highway. He played through situations in his head: What would happen if they pulled him over? How could he act in a more appealing way? Briani felt increasingly unsafe around police ever since Trump had become president. Because if he openly derided and threatened people who looked like her, what security did she really have? Like, if she was ever in trouble and needed to call 911, could she count on the police to protect her?

HEADLINES

June 1

NPR: "Peaceful Protestors Tear-Gassed to Clear Way for Trump Church Photo-Op"

June 2

The New York Times: "Holding It Aloft, He Incited a Backlash. What Does the Bible Mean to Trump?"

BRIANI

Killing Puppies

When she argued with her parents, they used it as evidence that Columbia had brainwashed her. It was frustrating, but she understood where they were coming from. It was that immigrant mentality: the desire to be grateful, assimilation as survival.

But look at Trump ordering the National Guard to tear-gas peaceful protesters so that he could stand in front of Saint John's Church and use the Bible as a prop!

That wasn't okay!

Briani asked her mom, "What is the worst thing that Trump could do to make you not support him?"

Because his comments about immigrants weren't bad enough.

And his comments about women weren't bad enough.

And his total disregard for the pandemic and just letting thousands of people die?

What was left? she asked. "Would it be killing puppies?"

Maia said there was a silver lining to all this. Without a racist-sexist-homophobe leading the nation through a pandemic and a low-key race war, the summer's racial-justice reckoning would not have happened. She hated to say it, but the country needed Trump.

Briani agreed, kind of. "I never truly accepted his presidency," she said. "But I've come to terms with the fact that he won, it happened, and this is what it brought."

For her, the silver lining was this: "For all the hate his presidency embodied, I saw so much love from people who saw that this was wrong and evil and wanted to do their part to fight against it."

GENEVIEVE

Complicit

It wasn't just a national reckoning. It was a personal one. Genevieve had spent two weeks after George Floyd's murder reconnecting with childhood friends, following the Facebook conversations unfolding among her high school class, journaling, and marching in the city. On the days she didn't go out, she'd be on her phone from the moment she woke up until the second she went to sleep. She'd forget to eat, forget to change out of her pajamas. It was stressful and painful and energizing all at the same time.

It boiled down to one question: Could she live in a racist and oppressive society and not be complicit? She knew a lot of people would say you can't be Black and racist. But this was her journey. This was the question she was asking of herself. It wasn't easy, but she had to do it.

For the first time, she was really interrogating colorism, the idea that the shade of your skin dictated how people treated you. She'd always thought of her skin tone as close to "cinnamon," which she knew—and had always known—had huge implications. Only now, she was really thinking about what those implications were.

Like in high school, her white peers would ask her what the "Black community" thought about this or that. "I saw this as my moment to shine and to be the spokesperson," she said. At the time, she didn't question why they were coming to her and not the other Black kids.

Or take dating. The way some guys in high school fetishized her—as "exotic" but light enough—was obviously racist. But she welcomed their attention, even reveled in it. She was a teenage girl and desperate to be seen as a romantic prospect. All of this hurt her darker-skinned friends. It was Genevieve implicitly saying, *It's okay to be interested in me and not them.*

To be 100 percent not racist, she would have had to reject these white friends, these boys. And that would have meant giving up any semblance of living a normal teenage life. She said that even her Black friends—the ones she'd hurt—understood where she was coming from.

That didn't let her off the hook.

But it showed her that "normal" was rooted in racism.

She'd spent all this time in wealthy, white communities. She saw how people's ways of existing were fed to them, taught to them.

That didn't let them off the hook, either. But it meant there was space for change. Maybe there was a way out.

Growing up, she often felt trapped in a kind of existential no-man's land. Everywhere she looked, it was either-or: Black or white, wealthy or not, city or suburbs, creativity or stability, Genevieve or Thandiwe. She didn't fit anyplace.

Now she wondered if the thing she hated the most was actually a kind of superpower. Her in-betweenness: the thing that allowed her to walk between worlds, keep her heart open and help others connect outside their silos.

CONNER

Sober

Conner had heard rumors of a Black Lives Matter protest in Springfield, but he was skeptical. The city was about 88 percent white, and 60 percent of residents had voted for Donald Trump in 2016. It wasn't quite as crimson as Ozark, more like a very deep rose.

Conner had also not watched the George Floyd video, but he'd gotten the push notifications on his phone and his high school friends had been talking about it on their group chat. They were all disgusted. And yet it felt far away. Far, because they lived in the southwestern corner of Missouri. Far, because they were, almost all of them, white.

Which made the scene at the corner of Glenstone Avenue and East Battlefield Road, right at the Battlefield Mall, so surprising. Conner and his high school friends, Taylor and Jack and Jack's little brother, were coming home from a secondhand bookstore called Hooked on Books when they ran into hundreds of people, most of them white, marching down the road with signs that read BLACK LIVES MATTER, I CAN'T BREATHE, and NO JUSTICE, NO PEACE.

They pulled into the mall parking lot. There wasn't much discussion. The next step was obvious. The four friends put on their masks, got out of the car, and joined the stream of protesters.

Who knew how long the march had been going by the time they arrived. But it just kept on, stretching for blocks down the central thoroughfare.

Conner's phone buzzed. Jacklynn was asking what he was up to. So he told her: *at the protest*. Which was probably a mistake, because she started freaking out. *What are you doing there?* she texted, her anxiety pulsating off the screen. *You're putting your life in danger.*

I'm not in danger, he said. *It's calm, it's orderly. I'm fine.*

My mom said they shut down the mall, she said. *They're worried about rioting and looting.*

Conner knew Sherry's heart was in the right place. Some of the people in his life (people he loved and respected) insisted on getting all their news from idiots. That wasn't Jacklynn. If anything, she was worried about the opposite thing: like the enormous truck adorned with Trump flags that sat menacingly in the middle of an intersection or the guy who later pulled his car into the stream of protesters, rolled down his window, and sprayed mace at them. Or the police themselves, who'd been doing terrible things to the marchers in New York.

But for the most part, everything here was peaceful. It was amazing to see.

Almost everyone wore a mask.

The police presence felt distinctly respectful.

Some protesters tried to calm down their angrier compatriots who were shouting "Fuck Twelve!"—aka fuck the police.

One protester even helped the mace guy navigate his way out of the crowd to try to de-escalate the situation.

Conner thought back to a climate protest he'd attended in New York the previous fall. He remembered kids there getting high and dancing to Jaden Smith. This, he thought, was different. It was sober. Sober in every way.

JACKLYNN

Come to Jesus

Jacklynn had been hanging out with her friend Bailey from work and a bunch of others and generally having a great time. But when everybody left, Bailey asked how things were going with Conner.

Before long, it all spilled out. How over quarantine they'd had all these come-to-Jesus moments, tear-filled emotional dialogues about how to fix things. But it didn't work. They'd grown too far apart.

Like on faith. They both hated organized religion, but as long as she could remember, Jacklynn had prayed to a higher power, to whatever was out there. But over time, she learned to keep this part of herself hidden. Because Conner couldn't abide by any of it. If you brought up God, he'd argue for rationality. Literally hours after her dad passed away, he'd tried to argue that heaven didn't exist! That left her stuck between a super Christian, religious family and a super atheist, antireligious boyfriend. At least if she needed to pray, her mother understood why.

But that wasn't even the most hurtful thing. A few weeks before her dad passed, Conner told her that she was only using him for emotional support.

Yes, she was emotional.

Extremely emotional.

But how could he say that? She'd tried, in every way, to show him how much she loved him. She'd made art for him, paintings and poems. She'd put him *in* her art, her deepest expression of love. She'd given him gifts, put tremendous thought into the details. And still, he didn't or couldn't believe that her love was real.

The relationship had become exhausting, Jacklynn told Bailey. She wasn't happy.

Bailey had just gotten out of a long-term relationship and said that what Jacklynn was describing sounded a lot like what had happened with her own ex.

And, all of a sudden, Jacklynn just knew. It was time.

When she got home, she told Sherry, who was shocked and worried about how it would impact both her daughter and Conner. But after Jacklynn had shared new details about the relationship, her mom realized it was time to move on. "I wasn't expecting this, but it sounds like you have your mind made up," she said. "There's nothing I can do to stop you."

CONNER

Exit Interview

It was about 1:00 a.m. and Conner was online with Jack and Taylor when Jacklynn texted. It was the second time that night he'd heard from her. Already, they'd argued about the afternoon.

How he'd been out with his friends instead of visiting her. Sure, he didn't see her as much as he wanted to, but he saw them *never*.

How he'd put himself in grave danger by attending the Black Lives Matter protest.

Her anxiety was out of control, and he felt solely responsible for keeping her brain and her heart steady. But no matter what he said or did, it was always, *You're not doing enough to calm me down, Conner. You're not showing enough affection, Conner. You're not there enough, Conner.*

Enough was never enough.

And so maybe he shouldn't have been surprised when they got on the phone and she said, "Conner, we need to talk."

"Okay," he said.

Jacklynn took a breath. "I've been talking to my friends and my mom. I think we need to break up."

"Okay." He listened, but he was having trouble processing. Was this actually happening?

"We've been fighting so much and for so long. Whenever one of us has a problem, neither of us is able to solve it, even when we try. It's just not working. I think we just have less in common than we did in high school. And our lives are so wrapped up in each other. I need time to work on myself. We need to offer each other space to grow."

What could he say? "I think you're right. And I appreciate how you're handling it. It's really mature of you."

"I want us to still be friends," she said. "I don't want to cut you out of my life."

Again, what could he say? "I agree."

"And Conner, next year when you're back at school, please go make some friends. You're in all these clubs and classes. You're a good person; you have every ability to do it."

Conner didn't know how to respond. He was trembling. Not angry, not panicking. Just . . . shaking.

I still want you in my life. You're a good person.

These were such clichés.

They said goodbye, hung up. Then he put on the science fiction film *Bicentennial Man*. The movie didn't do much for his sadness, but for a couple of hours at least, he was able to shut off his brain.

CONNER

Conner's Five Stages of Grief

— *Blindsidedness. Ever since they'd been fishing, things seemed to be on the up.*

— *Frustration. Because of how long and hard he'd worked to fix their problems without confiding in anyone. And yet the second Jacklynn decided to spill to her mom and friends, they convinced her it was time to quit.*

— *Reason. The balance between fighting and fun had been way off for a long time.*

— *Numbness. He was in too much shock to argue.*

— *Acceptance. He was kind of ready for it to happen, even though he didn't want it to. And he knew she'd been having a hard time because of her dad. The last thing he wanted was to make things harder.*

JACKLYNN

Aftermath

Jacklynn hung up and went to bed. She felt fine. But for the rest of the night, her brain kept kicking her awake. Every hour on the hour. *Remember what you did? Remember what you did? Remember what you—*

She woke up crying the next morning. She asked her mom if she'd made the right decision. Sherry assured her she had.

HEADLINES

JUNE 6

The New York Times: "Top Editor of Philadelphia Inquirer Resigns After 'Buildings Matter' Headline"

JUNE 7

HuffPost: "New York Times Opinion Chief James Bennet Out After 'Send in the Troops' Op-Ed"

JUNE 9

NPR: "Chief Editor at Bon Appétit Resigns After Racially Insensitive Photo Surfaces"

JUNE 10, 2020

The New York Times: "Condé Nast's Head of Video Resigns"

BRIANI

Pulling Teeth

Because of Black Lives Matter, white men were stepping down and media institutions were blowing up left and right.

The *Columbia Daily Spectator* wasn't about to make national news, but it wasn't immune. And Briani was in the middle of it. At the urging of her editor, she'd applied to become an editor herself. And that was the position she held when George Floyd was killed on May 25th and protests swept the country.

But *Spec* went on hiatus every summer. So *Spec* didn't immediately jump on the news. And from Briani's perspective, they didn't feel much urgency to do so.

Which didn't sit right with her, or her team at *The Eye*, among others on staff. That was a problem, because they couldn't start publishing stories without support from the Corporate Board.

The Corporate Board sounded scary and intimidating. It sounded white, wealthy, and male—i.e., corporate. In fact, it was none of those things. The Corporate Board, which included the *Spectator*'s editor-in-chief, its managing editor, and its publisher, were three female students of color.

Briani thought that these young women would have used their power to upend the status quo. She assumed that's what they'd want to do in solidarity with their sisters. But that's not what happened. People on staff told Briani that the Corporate Board had a way of changing you—a "power corrupts" scenario.

And maybe the status quo was partly to blame (e.g., *Spec* always took a summer hiatus), but so were the people in charge of setting it.

Briani didn't know anything about *Spec*'s history before she applied. She'd signed on with romantic notions: a supportive community of storytellers with a near religious calling to publish the truth. In fact, *Spec* had a reputation of being very white and very wealthy. Not just historically (because that was basically every student organization at Columbia) but currently. Briani had spent her first semester on staff more or less sheltered from this truth. *The Eye's* managing editor, Eve—Briani's direct boss—was a middle-class Black sophomore who was incredibly supportive of her trainees. *Spec*'s leadership was almost entirely POC. And these people had hired *her*—a young Latina woman—who'd devoted her application to the importance of representation. Also, the higher-ups talked a lot about their commitment to diversity and inclusion. The year before Briani joined, the paper had even conducted a survey aimed at revealing its blind spots. They'd found that only one member of the Managing Board was on financial aid.

Eve told her team at *The Eye* that after George Floyd's murder, she'd attended a meeting with the Corporate Board and each of the paper's section heads. She said the meeting had been incredibly frustrating: everyone angry and accusatory. She came away from the meeting feeling like getting the board to take decisive action was like "pulling teeth."

So on June 11th, the *Eye* team met to discuss all of this and how they, at least, could be more antiracist. Among the things they decided were:

— *Cover the protests.*
— *Hire more students of color.*
— *Better train reporters—even those of color—to stop tokenizing minority students in their stories.*

Eve went back to the Corporate Board with these ideas and found the leadership to be more receptive. In the end, *Spec* started a diversity, equity, and inclusion committee, but according to Briani, the leadership gave it little actual power. Eve said the problem wasn't a lack of power, exactly. "It was just putting more labor on a Black woman's shoulders," she said. The board effectively told her, Do whatever you want with the committee but good luck. Because she still had to run *The Eye* and she was shooting to become the paper's editor-in-chief. It was all too much.

Briani remained frustrated. "It's like I'm just an extra point for you to say you have a diverse staff. You have the power. I shouldn't have to tell you these concerns are legitimate."

JULY

BRIANI

Mask Mandate

Also like pulling teeth: getting customers to social distance when they came into the business. And as for wearing masks? Forget it. There was no mask mandate, and Briani feared people might get violent with her parents if they tried to enforce one inside the restaurant. She'd seen the viral videos of angry people assaulting store clerks. They were scary.

Of course, Covid was equally scary. But what choice did they have? The restaurant was the family's sole source of income.

In June, after searching for remote work and coming up with nada, Briani put on her face mask, grabbed some gloves, and headed over to the business to help out. Her brother was back to work at Chick-fil-A at the mall (where, Joseph reported, at least half the people walked around maskless or pulled their masks down to order). And Leonor and José needed help, especially now that in-person dining was back.

Leonor told her customers, "We need super limited capacity and social distancing. Six to ten people max. And we're only open from eleven a.m. to three p.m."

The customers told Leonor, Let us in! Why aren't you open? Why can't we sit down? Why won't you serve us?

Briani's job was to prep and pack the carryout orders and to sanitize everything in the restaurant. She used a diluted bleach spray on the tables and the menus, wiping every page of the menu multiple times. She never let a dirty menu touch a clean menu. She'd come up with a system to ensure that a dirty rag never touched a clean rag. All the while she was thinking, how did we *not* do any of this deep-clean sanitizing before? People's germs are so gross!

Meanwhile, there were always customers coming in—either to dine or to pick up their food. During the lunch rush, things got crazy, a pileup of people crowding around the register. No social distancing whatsoever.

Hispanic and white, it didn't matter. Briani said the Spanish-language TV stations were no better than Fox News, calling Covid a low-key hoax.

"We have to serve these people," she said. "We need the money. And it's hard because they genuinely do not care. They're being really selfish. We are literally risking our lives to serve you food."

CONNER

A College Try

Conner had a lot of downtime. School was over and he was jobless. He'd applied to the EntertainMart, the Hong Kong Inn restaurant, Family Video, and Barnes & Noble. No bites. He had intentionally *not* applied to Lambert's Cafe, a restaurant chain that had thrown open its doors to seemingly any and all job seekers—but also to the non-mask-wearing public.

So now he was holed up in his room and not doing much. He no longer had Jacklynn to talk to. He did not cry about it. He tried not to think about it.

He went on a couple of drives with Taylor and finally started to vent: about how she seemed to think every question he asked was teeing up an argument; about how he could never do enough, no matter how hard he tried; about how easily she seemed to be getting over him. It was the first time he'd ever opened up about the relationship to anyone. He'd wanted to talk to his friends over the years, but he knew Jacklynn would be offended if he shared their personal details. Doing it now felt clumsy, was perhaps fruitless, and yet he felt a little better knowing someone had heard him out.

He didn't tell his mom about the breakup right away. But Stacey had a habit of asking him what was wrong even when nothing was. She was a bit of a helicopter parent in that way. On this occasion, she just happened to be right. And so finally, after he'd rebuffed her a few times, she flat-out asked, "Did you guys break up?" And Conner said, "Yes, and I don't want to talk about it." And to Stacey's credit, she left him alone.

He met up with Jacklynn once for a post-breakup item exchange. She took back the hammock she'd bought him the day of their fishing trip. Conner took back *Stranger in a Strange Land*, which he'd given her and she hadn't read. Just before they said goodbye, Jacklynn gave him an old comic that belonged to her father, which she'd found in the garage. She thought it would be a nice gesture.

Mostly, he felt her absence. Her absence on the phone, her absence on Skype, her absence in their *Minecraft* world. In some ways, his future was blank.

Had his relationship prevented him from being more social? He didn't think so. Yes, he'd left Board Game Club early when she was having that crisis about her dad. And yes, he'd turned down that girl in University Writing who invited him to the Elizabeth Warren event. Maybe there'd been a few other instances. But he didn't consider any of them defining.

"There was never a moment where it was either 'talk with my girlfriend or go out and do something,'" he said. "Without Jacklynn, I would have had more time that I spent alone or just working."

Jacklynn had often suggested that he try harder to make new friends. In fact, long before their breakup, he'd pledged to work on this. He hoped to have a more social fall. But it was hard to think about any kind of fall without Jacklynn in the picture, just as it was hard to think about a fall semester in the middle of a pandemic.

"I don't one hundred percent know what trying harder means," he said. "But I have planned on it."

JACKLYNN

Movie Moments

Jacklynn and Conner had plenty of movie moments during their three-year relationship. When he came home early for winter break and surprised her at the bowling alley where she was playing with friends. When he'd planned one heck of a junior year promposal. When he brought her the personal pizza after her dad died. But what about all the movie moments she'd never had? The ones she'd missed, being in a long-term relationship?

For instance: those montages of best friends driving together, wind-swept smiles and ponytails flying. Best friends drinking shakes, their bare legs stretched across picnic blankets. Best friends goofing around at the mall, the ice cream shop, the lake.

The day she went out with her work friend Bailey and Bailey's friend Sidney felt like that. She was aware that she was living a movie moment, because she'd never had a day so perfect before.

The three of them went to Grant Beach Park in Ozark, to a spot memorializing a high school classmate who had passed away. There were hammocking polls. Jacklynn had never been hammocking. So she hitched up the one she'd bought for Conner and since retrieved. Then she sprawled out on the multicolored fabric and swung, staring up at the sky.

Then they hopped back in Bailey's Ford SUV and drove around

before parking at the James River Church. It was nighttime by then and the church was deserted, but the lawn sprinklers were on. At Bailey's instigation, they shucked off their shoes, hopped out of the car, and ran through the water, bracing and cold. They let the grass stick to their legs, sang Doja Cat at the top of their lungs. Maybe it was sacrilege, but Jacklynn didn't think Jesus or any other heavenly power would mind.

Then they were off to Springfield, to a little nothing of a park in the middle of the city. They ran up the hill to where the playground was perched and hopped on the swings, still sun-warmed, pumping, higher and higher, like they hadn't since they were little. They pumped through the dark, looking out over the neighborhood trees. The moon rose huge above them and Jacklynn flung her head back so that the cool light bathed her like a personal halo.

After this, they drove to Springfield Lake, where they sat on the rocks and looked out at the water.

They finished the night with ice cream, Jacklynn savoring her Oreo cheesecake shake.

They'd been out for nearly ten hours.

After her father, after Conner, she felt like she'd been waiting for things to get better. She felt like they never would. But they had.

Jacklynn posted photos of the day on Instagram. *Slowly but surely falling in love with life*, she wrote.

BRIANI

Low Point

Financial aid is a roller coaster. Approach the ride from below, and you see this large labyrinthine structure full of twisty rails and endless loop-d-loops. Your stomach drops before you even step foot on the thing. Briani had been riding the apparatus for over a year now. On a regular roller coaster, the more times you rode the ride, the less scary it became. You started to anticipate the treacherous climbs and precipitous drops. The whoosh in your stomach, so intense the first time, mellowed out with each turn.

Not so with financial aid.

For one thing, Covid made the ride scarier and more unpredictable. She'd applied for a summer earnings waiver, which would exempt her from the $2,300 that Columbia expected her to pay with summer job earnings. She'd spent weeks looking for remote work to no avail. And when she finally started taking shifts at the business, it was really to help her parents. They couldn't pay her nearly enough money to cover the fee.

The situation reminded Briani that the need for a paying summer job was one of those small but consequential obstacles that separated the experience of a low-income college student from the experience of a more privileged one. Kids who didn't need to make money over the summer—whose parents could help them afford the expenses of a nonpaying internship—could devote their break to following their passions and building professional relationships. That was harder if you had ambitions in law or journalism or design and, instead, had to work minimum wage at the mall.

And right now, there wasn't even that. So for weeks, Briani's anxiety climbed ever higher, as she awaited the school's verdict. Because what if they didn't grant the waiver? How would she cover the fee? She had no idea.

By midsummer, it seemed her anxiety had reached its apex.

Her financial aid letter arrived.

Hallelujah, her waiver was approved.

But holy shit! Her stomach lurched into her throat, her entire body slamming against the force of gravity as she dropped, down, down, down.

Because the letter said she needed to earn three grand during the next academic year. And how was she going to do that? Briani had secured campus housing for first semester. But the chance of her staying for the year? Slim.

"They told us to only bring two suitcases," Briani said. "If we have to leave because of Covid, we'll only have forty-eight hours to get out."

In that event, the university said they'd give students money for housing, but it wasn't nearly enough to cover a semester's worth of rent in New York. So she'd have to return home. Again. And what kind of job could she get in Georgia? Minimum wage was a lot lower here than in Manhattan. She'd still be paid for *Spec*, but it was far short of what she owed for the year.

In an online chat for FLI students, someone recommended canceling your dining plan and diverting the money to other expenses. That stuck Briani as a great idea. It made all these contingencies seem workable. But the school told her that wasn't an option. "I might have to beg them," she said.

She was sick of this roller coaster. Really sick and tired of it. She'd been upbeat, positive for so long. But she was struggling.

Because of the pandemic,

and the protests,

and Governor Kemp,

and Trump,

and the selfishness of all the maskless customers,

and the uncertainty about sophomore year,

and the mixed messages from financial aid,

and constantly trying to remember how lucky she was, because lots of FLI students were struggling much more than she.

"I feel like a sham telling kids to come to Columbia," she said. "The school does virtue signaling for racial, socioeconomic diversity, LGBTQ. But what are you *doing* for these communities?" She sighed heavily. "I just want this to be over."

A moment later: "For all the frustration, I still have this weird love. I love the people, and the physical campus, and the memories and the home I've made there."

A moment after that: "Just rip off the Band-Aid, and tell us we can't come back."

AUGUST

From: Lee C. Bollinger officeofthepresident@columbia.edu
Date: Fri, Aug 14, 2020, at 2:01 p.m.
Subject: [President-incoming-students] Update on the Fall Term

Dear fellow members of the Columbia community:

. . . Though six weeks ago we thought that we could safely house 60 percent of Columbia College and Engineering undergraduates in our residence halls, today we have concluded that we must drastically scale back the number of students we can accommodate in residence on campus . . . to those without access to stable internet, quiet study space, and other prerequisites for remote learning . . .

With few undergraduate students living on campus, we have decided that all undergraduate courses will be virtual . . . There will still be the chance to learn from some of the finest minds and teachers in the world and to experience the dazzling creativity that marks a truly outstanding university such as Columbia . . .

Sincerely,
Lee C. Bollinger

CONNER

Dungeons & Dragons

Conner was fairly certain Columbia would have let him back on campus, at the very least because of his unreliable internet. But he couldn't imagine paying for a plane ticket, simply to sit in his dorm room and do the same work he could do here.

And if he stayed in Missouri, the school would give him his housing allowance as a check—more than enough to cover his annual student fees. And good thing, because he still hadn't been able to get a job.

If he stayed in Missouri, he'd be near his friends.

If he stayed in Missouri, he'd be with his family.

It was a big silver lining to an otherwise downer of a situation.

And things at home weren't bad. Their grandfather had bought Ayden a small 3-D printer, and Conner had been helping him make Dungeons & Dragons miniatures, like the barkeep at an inn or a warlock wearing a top hat. He'd gotten his brother into comic books and even compelled him to start reading *Ready Player One*. (This was in exchange for a BB gun, but a win's a win.)

And an even bigger win: In early August, after years of not working, his mom landed a sales job at Bass Pro Shops. Stacey had told Conner that she was tired of staying home, tired of feeling useless. Tired of feeling anxious about her uselessness. Conner protested: *You're not useless! You're our mom!* But this was a big deal. They'd have dental and vision insurance, everything.

Conner promised to help her learn the store's computer system. He was relieved there was finally a mask ordinance.

Over the last few days, the house had felt empty and strange without his mom there, but it was also a return to their younger years, when his mom was healthier and had worked at Chase Bank and a local copy shop. Conner and Ayden would goof around and eat cereal out of a large mixing bowl. Now they would cook together—mac and cheese, buffalo dip, and egg sandwiches. Then at night when their mom walked in the door, they'd yell hello from across the house and ask about her day.

Stacey still had good days and bad days. But at the moment, the bad days weren't super alarming. And the thing is, Conner could be there to help. He could lighten the mood, get his mom and brother out of their heads. The three of them ate dinner together every night, usually in front of the living room TV: Adyen and Stacey on the overstuffed brown couch and Conner on the floor between them. After that they'd either keep watching their movie or play a game. He'd even introduced them to D&D, which he never imagined they'd play as a family.

Conner, of course, was the Dungeon Master. "Okay," he'd said the first time they embarked on their quest. "So you're on the road to see the king, and you're walking by the home of Farmer Maggot."

"Can we go to the farm?" Ayden had asked.

Conner paused. He didn't consider it an especially pregnant

pause, but his mom and brother thought otherwise. Like he was trying to intimate something.

"Can we go?" Ayden repeated.

"Are we supposed to go?" Stacey asked.

"I want to go," Ayden said.

"You do what you want to do," Conner replied, trying to remain neutral in his Dungeon Master role. In fact, there was no good reason to stop at the farm, but his family had already decided otherwise. "Farmer Maggot's hiding something," Ayden said, and he burst into the farmhouse and began digging through a random chest. Conner was laughing, thinking, *You are such a goober, Ayden.* But he was now on the hook to have Farmer Maggot respond to this unprovoked property violation.

"Hey!" Conner said, putting on Maggot's gruff voice. "Why are you digging through my stuff?"

Ayden reached for his sword, said he was going to fight.

Finally, Conner broke character. "Look, guys, if you fight Farmer Maggot, you're not going to survive." Because a few rolls of the die had already revealed that Farmer Maggot had seven sons, who were all armed with pitchforks and crossbows. Maybe if Conner could make the situation very intimidating, his family would get the memo: *Let's move along, already.*

But they were determined. Ayden began swinging his sword at the farmer, and Stacey started casting her witch's bolt at his sons. Soon Conner had totally lost control of the situation. It was a free-for-all bloodbath of weapons and sharp-pronged garden equipment and newly invented reinforcements that Conner brought in to help his mom and brother not die immediately. Every now and then, Conner lied about the dice roll to keep his family breathing, which he'd never do with his friends, but seemed like the right decision in this case.

And by the end, Maggot's seven sons lay dead around the farm and his mom and brother were barely hanging on to their mortal coils. "Well," Conner said, "Farmer Maggot has lost his bloodlust and decided to give up the fight."

Ayden and Stacey looked at each other, as though to say *Yeah, we know.*

And so, even though the game had gone totally off the rails, Conner felt good. He'd upheld the Rule of Cool, the only Dungeon Master rule that really mattered: As long as players had fun, you'd done your job.

He felt good, because even if his mom had started out anxious or stressed, her disconnection and somberness had morphed into engagement and laughter. Conner felt good, because he knew that playing Dungeons & Dragons with his mom and goober kid brother could never have happened long distance, over a screen.

BRIANI

Matriculate

In high school, Alberto gifted Briani a wall-sized poster of the New York City skyline, and she hung it behind her bed. At the time, the decoration was aspirational; a picture of what she hoped to achieve. Today, amazingly, it represented her success. Even if she wasn't currently in Manhattan, she could look at that poster and know that she'd *earned* Manhattan. The panorama was her life.

One day in August, this poster was the backdrop for a Zoom meeting between Briani and a rising high school senior named Jamal. Briani had met Jamal through Matriculate, a mentorship program that connected FLI college hopefuls with current college students. They'd been chatting regularly since June. In the beginning, Briani helped Jamal build— and then narrow down— his college list. He wanted a name-brand school, which Briani understood. But she also wanted to help Jamal find the right fit. He was the son of Somali refugees and identified as Black and Asian. Like Briani, he was a first-generation college student who'd grown up in Gwinnett County. Like Briani, he'd carried a lot of responsibility from a young age and had a foreign-sounding name that didn't always make life easy in the South.

Briani was hoping to pass some of what she'd learned freshman year along to her mentee: namely, getting into a name-brand school wasn't a golden ticket. It could be wonderful, but you had to proceed with your eyes open. At the moment, Jamal's doubts were like a fog, clouding the view.

For instance, he was struggling with his essay for the Common App. "It's hard putting my personal challenges out there," Jamal said about the essay. "What if people don't understand?"

Since the seventh grade, Jamal had managed his family's finances—paid the bills and filed the taxes. Then in 2018, after a driver totaled his mom's car, Jamal was put in charge of buying the family a new one. Before long, he started to realize some things. First, the sales associates often stumbled over his name. And second, they were quoting him prices that seemed inordinately high.

So as an experiment—but also to simply make things easier—Jamal started making up American names on the phone. When he used last names like Roberts, Adams, Williams, and Davis, he was quoted prices that were four to five thousand dollars less than when he inquired about the exact same car with his Somali last name. In the end, he used the American name "Susan Davis" to secure a good price, made sure the salesperson put the quote in writing, and then went with his sister to complete the transaction in person.

The salesman could barely hide his fury. He tried to make up excuses, even tried to give them a scratched car. But Jamal stood his ground. In the end, his family drove off with their new car at the previously negotiated rate. The Susan Davis rate.

Jamal's takeaway was powerful: He would always face discrimination but, he said, "My name isn't something that will stand in the way of my future or career or goals. I can use their tactics against them."

Even so, Jamal worried that admissions officers wouldn't understand—or even believe—him. "What if they think my story is made up, as if this is a whole lie that never happened?" he asked Briani. "Would you expect this specific kind of micro-aggression if you haven't been through it?"

Briani remembered writing her own college essay. She'd written about the family tradition of eating Costco pizza on weekly Sunday shopping trips. With her parents' work schedules, it was the only time they were all together. The pizza came to symbolize their efforts—not just to provide for Briani and Joseph but to give them the privilege of happiness. The pizza symbolized both their sacrifice and their love. And yet Briani feared that admissions officers wouldn't understand. How could the people reading applications about all-state champions and award-winning teen scholars understand the significance of a slice of Costco pizza?

But her truth was her truth.

"You have to trust the process and trust yourself," she told Jamal. "This is your story. You don't have to prove yourself."

It wasn't easy for Jamal to simply accept this. "I had to sit down and channel her wisdom," he said. But he did. He told his story with confidence, knowing that Briani had his back. The clouds of doubt did not fully disperse, but they began to dissipate.

"He wrote from his heart," Briani said later. "That's something other kids can't replicate."

The following winter, Jamal would be accepted to Rice University, in Houston. When she learned the news, Briani's heart would swell, knowing she'd played even a small role in his journey. But he'd done something for her, too.

In Georgia's sweltering late August heat, disappointment and injustice had begun to feel almost sunbaked into Briani's skin.

She'd watched the pandemic put her parents at constant risk, serving customers who didn't seem to care.

She'd watched it destroy her freshman spring and strip away the prospect of a sophomore fall.

She'd watched police officers club marchers who looked just like her and Jamal, Genevieve, Alberto, and Maia.

With all of this, it was hard to feel hopeful. But then she'd hop on Zoom with Jamal. Maybe they'd work through the thesis of his essay or she'd give him a pep talk about confronting imposter syndrome (which, let's be honest, was also a pep talk for herself). And instead of feeling bogged down by disappointment, she'd be buoyed by a sense of purpose.

Because she and Jamal were making space where there had previously been none.

"This is so much bigger than me," she'd tell Jamal. "I think of my ancestors, my parents, the generations of students who follow. We are all worthy."

AFTERWORD: SOPHOMORE YEAR

JACKLYNN

Burial

These days, when Jacklynn considered her life, she felt like an outside observer. Like she was looking at herself through a window. Who was this person who no longer worked at Big Whiskey's but instead drove into Springfield to be a hospital pharmacy tech? Who was this graphic design major, working alongside pharmacy and medical students? She'd never climbed a learning curve so steep. Every day felt like her first, with a hundred moving parts. And yet, for the first time in a long time, she felt challenged in the best way.

And that wasn't all. She was back in school full-time, attending classes at the Springfield Campus of OTC. She'd gone from a five-minute drive to a thirty-minute drive, from a campus with two parking lots to one with eight. And like at all the local colleges, most students didn't care that much about Covid. They weren't social distancing. In fact, they were partying. At one point, Jacklynn got a call from the health department: Someone on campus had exposed her to the virus, which meant she had to quarantine for fourteen days . . . in her home, with her at-risk mother.

In some ways, she felt safer at the hospital. The Covid unit was at max capacity, but at least her colleagues took the pandemic seriously. At least there were strictly enforced precautions.

And school was . . . school. She was eager to get through it, to become a professional, already. She'd always planned on transferring from OTC to Missouri State after getting her associate's degree. Now she was considering night classes at Drury University, a liberal arts college in Springfield. That way, she could earn and save. She could afford to move in with her new boyfriend.

Because that had changed, too. His name was Michael, a guy she'd met briefly at a high school speech and debate competition. She'd never forgotten him: how friendly and loquacious he was, how much older he seemed than all the other kids. And then, years later and single, there he was on Bumble. She messaged him: *I know you.*

Michael seemed to work every job there was: volunteer firefighter and EMT, 911 operator, gravedigger, travel agent. They dreamed not of merely buying a house but of building one. *Minecraft* made real.

When they started dating, her family wouldn't stop making jokes: *If your new boyfriend is a gravedigger, maybe he should dig the grave for Dad's cremation box.* Jacklynn didn't find this very funny, but when she mentioned it to Michael, he said he'd love to help. So he did. They went to the cemetery, and Jacklynn stood by as he plunged his shovel into the earth. As he drew out the soil, one shovelful at a time, Jacklynn felt her own buried feelings rise to the light. She felt the tears rise up and cascade from her eyes as dirt cascaded onto the grass.

She cried because she'd always believed Kelly might stop using and get better.

She cried for the relationship she'd never had as a kid and the one she'd never get to have now.

She cried because she didn't hate her father as much as she'd thought.

She cried because she'd blocked him on Facebook. How cruel she'd been, though she was only trying to protect herself.

A few days after Michael had dug the grave, the family gathered again and lowered her father's remains into it. They'd put him in a wooden box, which Jacklynn had painted with images her dad would have loved: the Batman symbol, an Indian and a cowboy, and some lyrics from "Carry on Wayward Son," by Kansas. In a way, she was burying—had already buried—her old life.

The last time she'd reached out to Conner, she asked for the long-distance bracelets back. They were priccy. And, anyway, they'd never used them.

Conner said the bracelets were in New York, so he had no way to access them. She said she understood. She asked him a few other questions, how was he doing and all that. But he didn't have much to say, didn't seem especially eager to engage. It seemed that he was burying some things, too.

Her love was tilled in that soil. She hoped he knew that. She hoped it would help him grow.

CONNER

Contentment

Almost a year to the day after Columbia shut down, Conner pulled into his driveway. He'd just dropped Ayden off at a friend's house for a round of D&D. Conner had been taking care of Ayden a lot since their mom started working full-time. He drove his brother to school on the days school was open, helped him with homework, and encouraged him to read science fiction. As a result, he often missed class, which in turn set him back and put his sleep schedule out of whack. But he didn't mind. He was happy to see his mom working and his brother starting to socialize more. Ayden was about to graduate eighth grade and this D&D playdate was the first time he'd ever been invited to anyone's house.

Conner climbed out of the car and into the crisp spring air. The rain had just stopped, and everything was damp. A train whistle echoed through the trees, their leaves dripping. This was Missouri, the best of his state distilled into a single moment. And sure, half the time, the rain drew a burnt-sulfur smell from the streets and the many train crossings could make you insanely late. But that was okay. He'd take those frustrations in exchange for this contentment.

At the same time, he was ready for school to resume—for real and in person. During three remote semesters, the internet had proved a constant problem. It was either buffering or disconnecting. To speed it along, Conner would turn off his screen during lectures. But then it was easy to space out. He wasn't enthusiastic about listening to a professor a thousand miles away drone on for an hour, while periodically stopping to ask, "Hey are you still raising your hand?" to some kid who forgot to click off the Zoom "raise hand" feature, before the kid finally realized what was going on and awkwardly said, "Huh?"

Seminars were better. Conner had a few that he loved. His professor for Existentialism and Love in Literature, both taught largely in French, was interesting and passionate. He'd explicitly said, "I don't want you writing cookie-cutter, boring essays."

Conner was also starting to consider his major. He was well on his way to completing all the courses for anthropology and was considering philosophy. He'd figured out how to work the system so he could major in one of those and still take all the film classes he wanted.

But it wasn't all academics. Campus was calling.

"Of course, I haven't met anybody I consider a friend or much more than an acquaintance," he said. "That's largely on me."

It was the most overt acknowledgment he'd made to his social struggles, his desire, as Jacklynn had said, to try harder. He was disappointed that this semester hadn't really allowed for that. But he was confident junior year would be different. A million years ago during orientation, he'd visited the radio station, thinking he might get involved. He'd never pursued it. Now he'd been in regular communication with the student producers about becoming certified to be a host.

He was also looking forward to all the little things: scheduling time to do his laundry in a machine that wasn't broken, exercising on the campus treadmills, eating in the dining halls, exploring Central Park, attending Philo debates, and playing board games.

"I am in college and this doesn't actually feel like college," he said. "But I registered for housing. I will register for classes. I am looking forward to almost definitely, maybe, hopefully going back in the fall."

Writing the Memo

On an afternoon in March 2021, Briani stepped out of the Hungarian Pastry Shop holding a to-go cup of Russian coffee (espresso, cocoa, whipped cream) and a freshly baked croissant. Hungarian was a Morningside Heights institution: dim and crowded, the too-small tables covered with textbooks and plates of cherry strudel. But sitting inside a coffee shop during the pandemic wasn't the smartest move, even if the staff did take your temperature. And the sun was out—thank god—so Briani and her friends from Contemporary Civilization headed back to campus.

Spring in New York City was unpredictable. Despite the budding trees and sidewalk blooms, the winter chill frequently swept through. Which meant you soaked up the brightness when you could, even if it was blustery. They sat down on the Low Library steps and pulled their pastries from the crinkling paper bags. Briani bit into her croissant. Pure joy. She was back.

Like many FLI students, she'd received permission to return to campus for second semester. It was empowering, if a bit strange, to know that most of the people she encountered around school had the same cultural knowledge and experienced the same financial deficits as she did. She'd even written an article for *Spec* about the experience: "The New Columbia Bubble:

First Generation, Low-Income Students Form the Majority in Pandemic-era Dorms." One of Briani's sources said that she could finally relax, knowing that most people were like her.

That was the thing about being FLI; it wasn't a visible identity.

Briani conducted her days with as much normalcy as possible. Still, she missed what she called "the spontaneity of the mundane": running into friends around the campus, impromptu late-night feasts at JJ's, pulling up a chair to cram with classmates at Butler Library. When she first arrived on campus, she'd wanted one thing: to find a home here. Without realizing it, she had. "Before, I was trying to survive," she said. "Now it's like, I freaking go here."

This made all the difference.

Last year, she'd been a trainee at *Spec*. Now she was on the deputy board and a co-features editor at *The Eye*. She might even have a shot at managing editor of *The Eye* her junior year. More than anything, working on the paper had forged a connection to the school. The original publication was founded in 1877, and here she was in 2021, helping to shape its policies and its culture. She took this responsibility seriously. That meant speaking up when she otherwise would have kept silent.

First semester of Briani's sophomore year, a trans student of color had applied to *The Eye*. Briani was super impressed by their application—how they expressed themselves and their commitment to storytelling. She hadn't been at the student's interview, but later, on a Zoom call with the editors of *The Eye*, she learned that the student had flubbed one of the big interview questions.

Tell us about a recent magazine article that you read.

Briani remembered getting this question herself, how flustered she'd been, because she hadn't known to prepare for it. She remembered her answer, too. She'd talked about the hustlers story, but she'd mostly referenced the movie. Further, she'd said it was published in *The Atlantic* when it was actually published in *New York Magazine*. Afterward, her only thought: *I hope I passed their test.*

It made sense that *Spec* editors would want cultured, informed writers on staff. And even if there were some elitist assumptions that went into that (whose culture? informed about what?), the fact remained: If you were going to write for magazines, you needed to also read magazines.

Now, sitting on the other side of the table, she saw things differently. The interview question wasn't unreasonable. What struck her as unreasonable—as unfair, really—was to judge this candidate's entire application based on that single question. Because:

Having the time to read magazines was a privilege.

Having the money to subscribe to magazines was a privilege.

Having the courage to apply to a competitive student club, knowing that you were probably the only person who identified the way that you identified was a big deal.

And she'd flubbed her answer, too, and it hadn't hurt her prospects.

The Eye staff told the Corporate Board they wanted to hire the student. This was a different board than before: two white women oversaw editorial and a Black woman oversaw the business side. But according to Briani, the editorial leadership were skeptical about the new candidate.

Spec's leaders talked a big game about wanting more diversity on staff, Briani said. But when presented with a candidate who brought diversity on so many levels, who had tremendous potential—see: their top-notch written application—but didn't check every box, the Corporate Board wouldn't give that person the benefit of the doubt. The board assumed the candidate wasn't capable instead of assuming they were.

And how many others had been denied access to *Spec* for this exact reason? The next thing Briani knew, she was writing the Corporate Board a memo.

> As a person of color in *Spec*, and being FLI, I'm not going to weigh whether or not someone consumes the *New Yorker* or *The Atlantic* daily when their written application was good and they fumbled on their interview. Personally, I scarcely found time to read magazines ever because I was busy working at my parents' business and minimum wage jobs at the mall so I don't think it's fair for us as an organization to aspire to champion diversity, inclusion and equity and not give that same courtesy to people who perhaps do not have the resources or time to read magazines.

Even as she was typing, she thought, "Am I really about to do this?" Because it wasn't like her to be so forward, so overt. She'd always thought of herself as someone who let things happen—not someone who *made* things happen. In the past, she worried about the repercussions: getting a bad grade if she confronted her AP English teacher about the woman's racist reading of Ralph Ellison, or speaking up when that guy at the movie theater threatened her dad, or telling customers at the restaurant that they needed to wear their masks. In the past, she talked herself out of taking action. *Keep your thoughts to yourself. Don't stick your neck out. It's not a big deal.*

She kept writing.

> We know it might require more work on our ends but that's what we're willing to do, and I cannot in good faith and conscience penalize someone because they don't read *Rolling Stone* or subscribe to *Vulture* or *The New York Times Magazine*.

College had changed her. For the first time, she'd been around people who were more outspoken, people who had no problem saying, I'm not going to stand for this anymore. She was now one of those people.

Because while listening to the Corporate Board list all the reasons why they shouldn't hire the candidate, Briani realized, *How many times have I been the one who wasn't chosen? How many more doors would have opened if I'd been sitting in the room? Like I am now. And since I have some power—even a little—I also have an obligation.*

> I see where y'all are coming from but as someone from an underrepresented background and identity at Columbia and at *Spec* as a whole, part of being inclusive and

accessible is recognizing not everyone has access to these opportunities or resources or has the luxury of leisure or time to do so.

She finished the memo.

She told the board they could officially attribute all of this to her.

She hit send.

Acknowledgments

Rising Class **would not exist** without Briani, Jacklynn, and Conner. You guys are remarkable in so many ways. Your energy, passion, and honesty made this book a joy to report and write. I am excited to see where life takes you and the amazing things you will undoubtedly do. As Sherry says, you don't need to have it all figured out—but I know you *will*.

To Genevieve, Alberto, Marla, Maia, Jamal, and all the other friends in Lawrenceville and Ozark, thank you so much for sharing your perspectives, feelings, and opinions. Similarly, Sherry, Stacey, Leonor, and José welcomed me to their cities and into their homes. Of course, you already know that you've raised incredible kids who care for you deeply. As a mother and daughter, I understand that parent-child relationships are complex; I've tried to convey that complexity in these pages while never losing sight of your kids' love and appreciation for you and the sacrifices you've made for them.

Thank you to Joe Keohane for assigning the story, "Giving up on the American Dream," that inspired this book, and to its profile subject, Dajourn Anuku, for introducing me to the first-gen college experience.

I would like to thank the many college-access programs, along with deans at Columbia, Barnard, NYU, City College, Fordham, and others with whom I spoke while first embarking on this project. Of course, I owe a special thanks to QuestBridge, for introducing me to Briani and for your support of Conner (though journalist tip, I first encountered him via a Twitter post). Thank you to the many, many first-generation students I interviewed at Columbia and so many other schools back in 2018 and 2019, especially the leaders of Columbia FLIP. Every one of you deserves a book.

Jessica Goudeau gave me the confidence to break the rules—and it was absolutely the right decision. Sheri ArbitalJacoby double- and triple-checked. Thank you! To everyone at FSG, it's been a delight to have you on my team: Samira Iravani for the beautiful cover (and the many drafts); Sarah Gompper and free-lance copyeditor extraordinaire Jackie Dever for the careful read; Asia Harden and Hannah Miller for making the important things happen; Samantha Sacks, Mary Van Akin, and Morgan Rath for their killer game plan and genuine excitement for this book. To my amazing editor, Joy Peskin: I had never even heard of this genre when you first reached out to me but was immediately captivated by its power and the pureness of its storytelling. You've been a fabulous guide throughout this journey and, in the later stages, helped whip this book into shape. It's been such a pleasure to work with you, and I know we will again. Mollie Glick, it is exciting to be teaming up with you again after so long. You always fight for me, and I'm forever grateful.

I owe a tremendous debt of gratitude to Roy and Barbara Feifer, who thought they were taking us in for a few months and became our house parents for eighteen. This book would literally not exist without the space, and time, and childcare, and love you provided. (Extra thanks to Roy for giving up his office and for the Iron Man medals that reminded me daily to keep going.) To my parents, Aaron and Lindsay Miller, I owe so much of my success to your support, encouragement, and example. You wanted me to become a journalist and I did!

To Fenn and Collin. It's hard to imagine that I was dragging a breast pump around for half the reporting of this book. Now one of you is a legit child and the other is basically a teenager. I love you so much (even though I'm not sure you know what I do for a living). I cannot wait to see everything you boys do and become. Finally, to Jason, who I'm thrilled to say has just published his own book. (Way to catch up!) As usual, you weathered my anxiety and self-doubt with unfailing patience. For that, and for your love, I am especially grateful.

About the Author

Jennifer Miller is the author of four critically acclaimed books, *Inheriting the Holy Land*, *The Year of the Gadfly*, *The Heart You Carry Home*, and *Mr. Nice Guy*. Today Miller is a regular contributor to the *New York Times* and the *Washington Post*. She has reported extensively on teenagers and campus life and, more broadly, on disenfranchised communities, including military veterans, formerly incarcerated individuals, and the rural working class. She has taught undergraduate writing courses at Columbia and has been a thesis advisor at both the Columbia School of the Arts and the Columbia Journalism School. She lives in Brooklyn with her husband and two sons. byjennifermiller.com